GOLF *SWING* FROM THE GROUND UP

CHRISTOPHER AND GWENDOLYN WARNER

GOLF *SWING* FROM THE GROUND UP

Published by Tate Publishing & Enterprises, LLC
127 E. Trade Center Terrace | Mustang, Oklahoma 73064 USA
1.888.361.9473 | www.tatepublishing.com

Tate Publishing is committed to excellence in the publishing industry. The company reflects the philosophy established by the founders, based on Psalm 68:11,
"The Lord gave the word and great was the company of those who published it."

Cover design by Joel Uber
Interior design by Joana Quilantang

Published in the United States of America

ISBN: 978-1-62746-249-5
Sports & Recreation / Golf
14.03.24

CONTENTS

MY GOLF HISTORY

As a young man at the age of nine, I was introduced to the game of golf. I would caddy for my grandfather, Howard Pinner at a par-three course in Jacksonville, Florida. The holes ranged in distance from seventy-five to one hundred fifty yards. At that time, I thought that was big. My grandfather played with a foursome of railroad retirees that played every week on Tuesday morning at nine sharp. I wasn't really interested in the game at that time, I just wanted to get out of the house and spend time with my grandfather. I realized the fun they had, and the camaraderie they shared. I was not about to be left out. During the summer months when I was out of school, I would borrow my father's set of Kroydon clubs and fill in when there was a vacancy; and other times, we would even play with five of us. I didn't take the game seriously then, but I really enjoyed the time spent with my grandfather. I also went with my dad, Frank Warner, when he could break away from his 100-hour plus workweeks.

I continued playing through high school and on into my working days. My father, seeing the potential as well as the continuing growth of my game, would film my swing with his 8mm camera as an aid to help me with my mechanics. Again, I didn't take it very seriously, but it was nice to accompany friends as well as fellow workers in a round without embarrassing myself. I was soon introduced to a full-size course where using woods were part of the game, which changed everything. Realizing that a whole new swing was needed, I began to work on my new game. I would pay my $7 green fee, which was good for the whole day and play from sunrise to sunset. I didn't have the extra money for a cart, so I walked. There were times that I would play upwards of fifty-four holes in a day. When darkness fell upon me and I couldn't see where I was hitting the ball, I would decide to call it quits. My regular course was the Dunes Country Club in Jacksonville, Florida. Sadly though, it doesn't exist anymore. I soon gained enough skill and confidence to start trying new courses, and that's when things really started coming alive for me. I acquired an instructional video tape around 1984 titled *Golf My Way* by Jack Nicklaus. I practiced everything on the tape, attempting to emulate his every move and follow his direction. It was then that I began to understand the fundamentals of the swing. Although I have purchased a vast number of additional instructional videos over time, I believe that *Golf My Way* was the most influential one of all. I acquired multiple golf instructional books as well. My golf buddies and I purchased American Heart Association annual cards, which entitled us to play various courses around the state of Florida. We really enjoyed that. In addition, they were able to line me up three years in a row to participate in marshaling the TPC at Sawgrass, Tournament Players Championship. We were able to play the tournament course after the event in return for volunteering all week. Playing the Stadium Course was a memorable experience. I spent time practicing my short game in the yard behind the house. During that time—1988—my five-year-old daughter, Jessica, being curious and eager to understand what her daddy was doing, tried showing me her swing. I took a junior club, cut it down to her size, and used some tape for a grip. After taking a moment to position her and show her a few things, she was quickly hitting balls across the backyard. Although those days are long gone, she still retains everything I showed her. In 1990, my wife and I went separate ways.

I ended up moving to Houston, Texas in 1995, and soon began a new career with an airline working on the ramp in the main hub at George Bush Intercontinental Airport (IAH). I worked my way up to a hub manager. In 1996, I purchased my first new set of Spalding clubs right off of the store shelf. They weren't the greatest, but they were the best I could get at the time. I started playing a little more often, but still juggling a busy schedule at work, it was only leisure golf. In 2001, the best thing in my life happened to me. I met my present wife Lyn whom also worked for the same airline. She encouraged me to play more often; and with her having two sons from a previous marriage, I had the pleasure of introducing them to the game. They caught on real quick, and I soon had golfing partners again. The best part of it all is that my wonderful wife realized my passion for the game and continuously pushed me to play more. I definitely owe my certifications and accomplishments to her. Where I wanted to put the game aside and work two jobs all of the time, she refused to allow me to do so. She always supported me and encouraged me in every way. She also witnessed the culture that the game promotes and instills in young people. It became a win-win situation for us all. As a family, we joined Hearthstone Country Club and played a whole lot of golf. The boys were able to play even when I couldn't. When 911 happened, we like a lot of other individuals throughout the country were effected financially and were forced to prioritize things and give up the membership. However, before too long we were able to resume playing on a regular basis. I was also able to purchase some nice Callaway X 16 clubs, which helped improve my game. I joined the Player Development Program (Players Club), at Longwood Country Club in Cypress, Texas. I soon upgraded my clubs again to Ping G5 irons, but this time I had them custom fitted and special ordered. I gave my set of Callaway irons to my younger son Lance Lemmons, and purchased some nice Cleveland clubs for my eldest son Clayton Lemmons. We began enjoying the game once more. In addition, I joined High Meadow Ranch Country Club in Montgomery, Texas, and even competed in an OB Sports tournament. I spent thousands of hours on the range, working with all of my clubs. This was one of numerous tournaments that I participated in at multiple levels.

Through all of this, I discovered that I couldn't keep to myself while on the range when seeing someone else struggle with their attempt to enjoy the game. It was like bad music; even if I wasn't touching it, it hurt to see. By nature, I tend to want to lend a helping hand in all that I do. What seemed to be foreign to others was simple to me. This told me a lot about myself and where my true calling was, so I decided to get my certification as a professional instructor. I acquired a certification with the National Registry of Professional Golf Instructors. Soon my wife and I purchased a wonderful home right on the golf course at Houston National Country Club near Cypress, Texas. I even took a part-time job in the pro shop. Interested in continuing my education and certification process, I attempted my first Player Ability Test for my Professional Golfers' Association (PGA) card at South Shore Harbor Country Club in League City, Texas, and was successful in passing. It was a very cold and windy day, to say the least, but something went right. I continued moving forward with my certification process, and received my second certification with the United States Golf Teachers Federation. I continually advanced with them until I reached the highest level—being a Level IV Master Teaching Professional as well as a certified and licensed examiner. I started a professional golf instructional certification school as an organization working with other teaching professionals. To learn more about the organization or seminars, go to www.golfteachersacademyofamerica.com.

I continue to spend countless hours practicing, reviewing instructional videos and reading new material, conversing on forums and sharing ideas with other professionals, with a strong desire to continually improve my skill level and teach others. With a quest to reach new heights and shoot for the stars, who knows what the future may hold!

THE BEAUTY OF GOLF

Golf is not only a game for life; it's a game of life. Also, it's an opportunity to show ones inner self, and is the one independent sport that is immune to the performance of others. It reflects the level of dedication through performance and ultimately displays ones character that only circumstances reveal. Everyone loves to experience great shots and produce an impressive score. Looking good in front of others seems to solidify their confidence level. It's the undesirable shots though that gives one the chance to display their self-control, and view of how adversity should be handled. However; it's not about adversity, it's about recovery and how one conducts themselves when things don't happen as they prefer. This is usually a time when one's guard is down and their true feelings are easily unleashed.

Golf is a game that has intrigued mankind for centuries. It actually started as a game by the Romans; much like golf, one would strike a feather-stuffed ball with branches that were shaped like clubs. The Dutch played a similar game on frozen ice around the fifteenth century, which over time evolved into a sport more as we know it today. In fact, in 1457, golf was even banned in Scotland; because it interfered with the practice of archery, which was crucial to the country's military defense. Nevertheless, the Scotts continued playing the game on seaside courses referred to as links. Scotland proudly boasts the oldest golf course being Saint Andrews, which was used as early as the sixteenth century. As Golf made its way to the United States, the first eighteen-hole course was founded in 1893, and was known as the Chicago Golf Club. Since that time, we have seen an untold number of changes in the game of golf. With the advantage of science and technology, golf has been and continues to be an ongoing feat.

On January 17, 1916, a department store manager Rodman Wanamaker hosted a luncheon for a group of New York area golf professionals and well-known amateurs, which was held at the Taplow Club in New York City. Their purpose was to discuss the idea of forming a national association that would promote interest in the game of golf. It was also an attempt to elevate the vocation of golf professionals. They would meet during the next several months; and on April 10, 1916, the PGA of America was officially formed with the thirty-five charter members signing the constitution and bylaws. Their purpose was to promote enjoyment in the game, which would include the general public. It would also contribute to the growth of the game by producing services to golf professionals. By enhancing the skill levels of the PGA professionals, it would expand playing opportunities for the general public, employers, and manufacturers.

On March 22, 1934, the first Masters Tournament was played in Augusta, Georgia. The tournament was actually called the Augusta National Invitational until 1939. This was a course designed and brought into existence by the great Bobby Jones. The Masters soon became one of the four majors on the PGA Tour. The other three majors are the US Open, the British Open, and the PGA Championship. Since then, the Masters has become the premier stage for the greatest names in golf. It is played in the spring of each year, when the azaleas are in full bloom and the course is in its peak condition. The pinnacle in a professional golfer's career is the opportunity to proudly slip into the green jacket, and have their name permanently engraved into history. All of the majors have their level of glory and the ultimate dream is to accomplish the grand slam by winning all four in any given year. The world of golf is ever changing, and new talent presents itself each season. Technology and equipment continues to advance and courses are responding by lengthening the yardages as well as creating more challenging designs.

THE TRUE ESSENCE OF GOLF

Since the beginning of time, man has competed amongst one another in numerous ways. The quest for reaching new heights as well as outperforming the competition has developed an insurmountable drive to dominate a subject of interest. Where some sports activities are dependent upon a team of individuals working together as one with a common goal, golf is a sport in which each person is responsible for their own success or failure. With this in mind, the individual spends time and money attempting to gain an advantage by any means available. This is an ongoing feat in which marketing gurus utilize their skills, and capitalize on the opportunity to satisfy the hunger of the ever-growing population of golf fanatics. In today's society, research and technology offers a shortcut for everything. If a person has a particular fault, there is a special tool or club to compensate for it. This however, being thought of as a technical advancement or breakthrough, is actually a bandage for the incorrect execution of the task at hand. People in general seem to excuse their deficiencies and faults by blaming the equipment or the conditions of the course. Knowing that, multiple manufacturing companies thrive on the fact that the person will be continually in the market for the ideal "fix." When it comes down to facing the real problem, however, the true fault lies with the person, due to improper technique and process. With that in mind, it is a proven fact that those who are willing to face the truth and take the necessary steps to correct their mistakes are the individuals that seem to continually advance in their skill level and reach a higher level of performance and enjoyment.

This book is dedicated to those individuals seeking a deeper understanding of the correct way to perform a mechanically sound and smooth swing. It is also a tool for those who want to build a functional and usable strategy, while enabling them to navigate any golf course based on its particular characteristics and layout. A famous quote by Bobby Jones once stated that "the hardest course that one can encounter is five inches, which is between the ears." Golf is a sport in which each and every shot can be advantageous or disastrous. The player needs to accept the fact that the only important shot is the shot ahead of them. Remember, golf is played one shot at a time. The time to analyze the outcome is at the conclusion of the round. It is also crucial that the player doesn't dwell on the previous shots, despite the quality or outcome. What's done is done, and it can't be changed. Golf is a sport that is played in the mind and executed through the body. After all, the mind tells the body how and when to make certain movements. It's also where the senses are processed. Our confidence level depends on how we feel about our ability to succeed or fulfill any task, which will determine whether we will truly commit to the action. If one analyzes their options, taking in as much information as is available, then commits to the shot and finally attempts to execute it, they have done all they can do. If the particular shot produces unfavorable results, it is then that they continue the learning process, make the necessary adjustments, and enable themselves to grow and achieve a higher skill level. If the shot produces favorable results, it too can be a learning experience. Remembering the things that were done correctly can be as beneficial as those that were not. This is how we continually "find" ourselves and determine our limits and capabilities. If one is willing to work on the things within their control, and accept the things that are not, they will experience the highest possible level of performance and indulge in the true enjoyment that the sport has to offer.

INTRODUCTION TO GOLF

Golf! What a great game. It's known as the one unsupervised sport that allows you to take your character and place it on a stage for everyone to see. It's also a game with virtually an unlimited number of choices.

After all, no two shots are exactly the same. Knowing that, we spend time at the practice tee rehearsing what we're going to do when we actually get out onto the course. I've been playing golf since 1970; and one thing that I've certainly learned over the years is that some things never change. I'm basically referring to the average recreational, occasional, or weekend golfer. They'll typically get to the course and do one of two things. The first individual will show up right at tee time, grab their equipment and check in, run out to the first tee and start playing.

For the most part, it reflects in their score. They use the first nine holes to warm up and blame their bad shots on it. The other individual who gets to the course early enough will head to the practice range to get started. They'll usually go through a few motions appearing to warm up. They might even take a moment to stretch and take a few practice swings.

But then the next thing you know, they're teeing up; then heading for their bag and inevitably pulling out, you guessed it, the driver.

Then they'll start trying to hit balls to the back of the range.

Though they might hit a nice shot here and there, the majority of their shots will be topped, sliced, hooked, and basically sprayed all over the place. When they can't get any consistency they just call it a bad day. After a short time they'll reduce down to the irons, trying different shots by seeing what each club will do and how far each club will go, and that's about as far as they go with it. The next thing you know, you look up and they're gone. Does that sound familiar? Keep in mind though, it's like anything else; you usually get out of it what you put into it. The problem with most golfers is that they have no idea about proper mechanics and how to apply them to their swing. They don't know how to practice with purpose, and fail to realize just how important it is. Just going to the range and hitting away is unrealistic and will get you nowhere. So with that, I ask, "Are you ready to take your game to a whole new level?"

I'm Chris Warner, master golf teaching professional and certified examiner; and welcome to *Golf Swing from the Ground Up*. Whether you're a seasoned golfer wanting to tune up your game or brand new to the sport and not sure just where to start, this book is exactly what you need to help you reach your goals.

Now there's a lot of information out there, which can be quite confusing. For instance, there are a lot of golf instructional DVDs on the market. However, they are usually game or subject specific. This simply means that the content of each video covers a portion or specific subject. If you want the entire game, you'll end up having to buy a whole series, and that can get rather expensive.

Over the years there have been a lot of books published about golf.

The majority of them have a lot of great information in them; but if you're like most people, you learn much easier by hearing and seeing, rather than reading. The student can actually see the end result, removing the translation factor, which becomes reassuring. With this in mind, I have added multiple pictures to assist in seeing and understanding the information in this book. This is in an attempt to make you feel as though you are actually in the situation yourself. Now, we're all familiar with those monthly magazines that are out there, which usually have several pages of instructions and private lessons and so on.

And there's actually some good information in those articles as well. The problem that novice golfers have is that the advice in those articles is usually exaggerated in an effort to emphasize specific movements and actions. People in the learning stages tend to take those suggestions very literal, so they end up making changes in their swing and getting even more confused.

There are a lot of training aids on the market that are designed to guide and develop body movements so that the student will acquire the feel of making a proper movement and be more aware of their fault. My belief though, is if they're not careful they will develop a dependency on them. Each individual processes information differently, and has their preferred technique in learning, or style. The four main learning styles are: visual learners (which are acquired through observation), auditory learners (processes information heard), kinesthetic learners (hands on), and the thinker (sees things through a technical point of view). Most individuals have a combination of learning styles, but will find that one will be dominant. One is not better than the other, its a genetically individual characteristic. Now when all else fails there is that person in your group.

You know the one! They're the expert that can tell you everything that's wrong with your swing, but they sure struggle with their own. Where they're trying to give advice and help you by suggesting all kinds of different things, they're only adding to the confusion and frustration. Friends, it doesn't have to be that way. All you need to do is learn the basic fundamentals and how to apply them to your swing; and you'll have much more success. So, if you're ready to have some fun and enjoy the game as it was intended, come with me on a journey and let's build your golf swing from the ground up.

This book is the result of giving thousands of lessons and clinics, as well as countless hours of research about the fundamentals and mechanics of the swing. It also covers the most effective ways of teaching and motivating other individuals. I've accumulated a library of data and information, which has added to my appreciation and knowledge of the game. I've taken that information, and put it together to build a complete understanding and learning strategy, which I'm going to share with you in this book. Golf doesn't have to be a confusing task, the more you know about it, the more you can actually enjoy it.

The chapters in this book were written in a progressive order which should carry you through to the next step. I highly recommend that you don't skip through any chapters, especially the first time reading this. Doing so will only slow down your progress, which could prevent you from reaping the full benefits of what this book has to offer. Now I could spend a lot of time sharing what people do wrong in the swing; but we would be here all day, and it would just become confusing. My desire instead is to show and explain to you the correct way to perform the swing, and how to achieve great results. Think about it like this. Building your swing is like building a new home. You could have the best looking house on the block, but without a solid foundation you will always have problems. Building a great golf swing is like learning to ride a bicycle. By learning it correctly the first time, you'll never have to learn it again. My intentions in writing this book were to take the golf swing and break it down into a simplified version so everyone could relate to the game regardless of their skill level. I included as much of the verbiage commonly used in golf, so that when the reader hears the phrases, they'll have a clear understanding of how they apply. I also used multiple correlations with items people are familiar with in comparison to the movements described in the swing. This seems to make the translation of information much easier. I have taught thousands of individual students of all ages and skill levels, both male and female, given many large and small clinics, taught night school classes, worked with high school teams, and performed inspirational seminars for other teaching professionals throughout my career. With the experience that I've gained from this, along with years of research and success, I have brought it all together and put it in this book for the benefit of all individuals desiring to learn or improve the quality of their game. So with that, let's get started.

THE GRIP

I purposely started with the grip, because I believe that it's the single most important element in the golf swing. If you think about it, it's the only thing touching the golf club. Remember, the club has no idea how experienced or inexperienced you are. It only reacts to forces applied to it, and it simply goes where it's directed. Keep in mind though, if the grip is incorrect, it sets you up for failure right away. It's important that you get the grip right. I cannot stress it enough!

Now, I'm a right-handed player; but if you're left-handed, the same principles apply, just the opposite. But for the sake of confusion, I'll refer to the forward hand as the hand closest to the intended target. As a right-handed player, that would be my left hand; because as you can see, I hit toward the left.

That's also the hand that initiates the grip. Although there are three basic or common grips, this part is consistent with all of them. Now, there are countless opinions on the proper grip; but I'm going to share the easiest way to get it right, and I'll explain why it is right. I've found this to be extremely successful with all of my students. They seem to get the grip correct every time; and when they get the proper sensation, it sticks with them.

Holding the club straight up, you can place the forward hand on the club so that it's held using the last three fingers, as such.

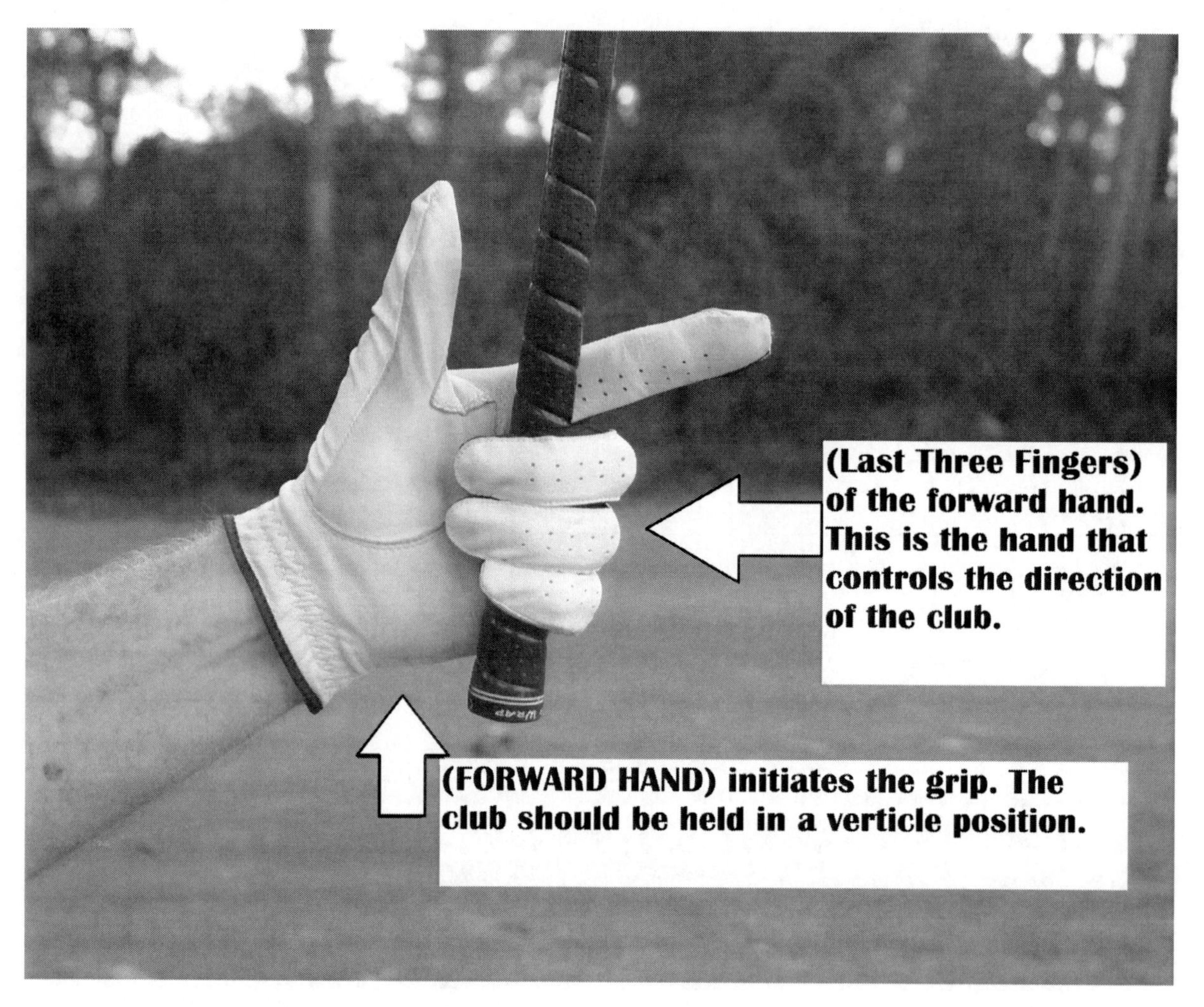

Once you get the club into position, take the club, and hold it straight in front of you as though you were going to use it as a hammer.

Find the point where it feels the strongest by making a hammering motion. If the club is held in the weak position, which is turned outward, it actually hurts. It tends to apply significant stress and isolates the thumb. Now if you hold it in the stronger position, which is turned too far inward, this will significantly reduce the range of motion, which will prevent you from properly cocking and releasing the club in the swing. The reason this is important is you're actually going to be making a sideways, hammering motion in the swing.

The 90 degree angle
that is established
between the (forward)
arm and the club, are
similar to cocking and
swinging a hammer.

Cocking a hammer is
similar to cocking a club
in the backswing. The
area between the thumb
and index finger (V) is
on top.
Similar to a club,
the hammer is
controlled by the
last three fingers.

This will also put your dominant hand in the position to properly cock, or release the club in the backswing. When the club is in the address, or hitting position, the hands will also be correct on the club.

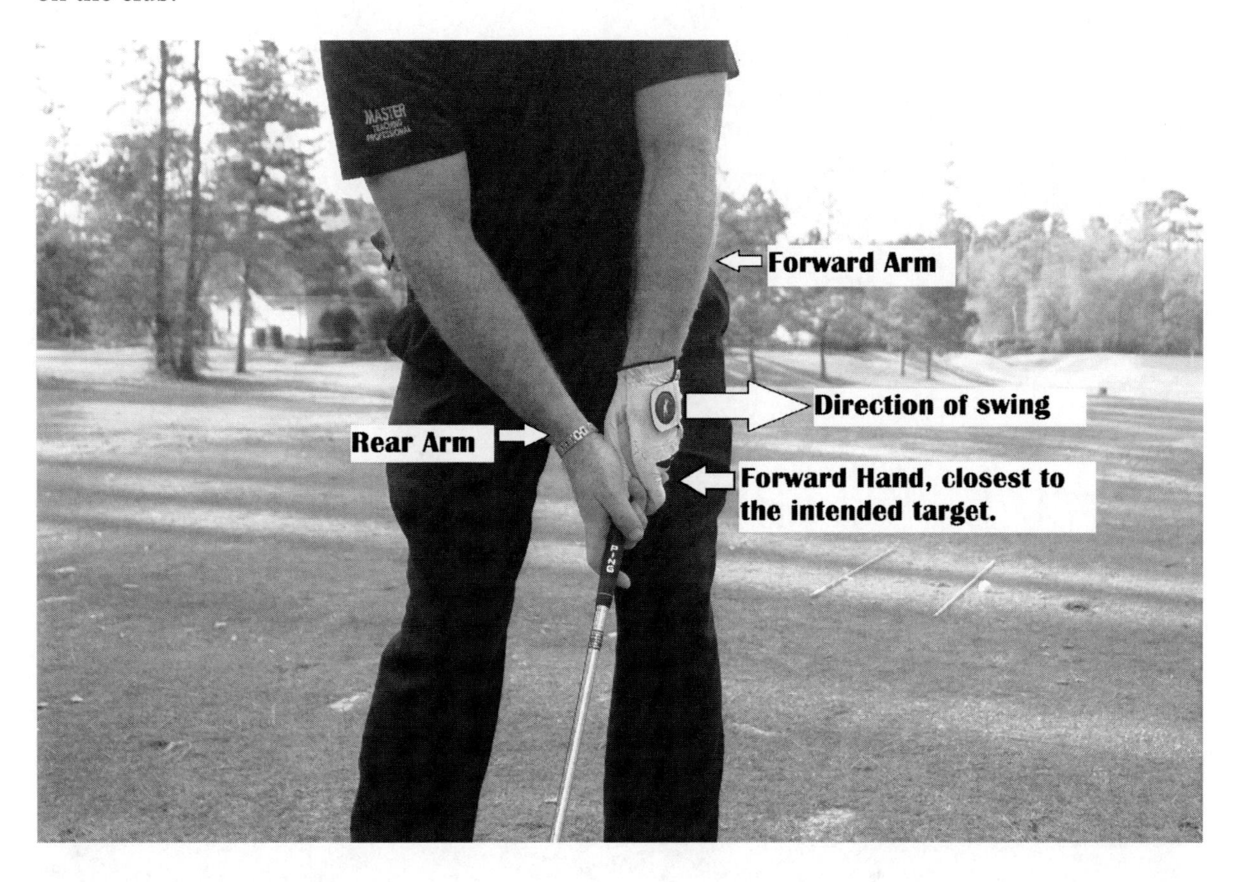

Once the forward hand has taken its place onto the club, the index finger should gently lie onto the club; and the thumb should do the same, but on the opposite side. The gap between them should be closed. Now, this is the point in time that you need to decide which grip you want to use. If you haven't already established one yet, I suggest that you experiment with each one to find what works best. Each person has their preferred method based on what feels most comfortable, and that's important because comfort promotes consistency. It also helps alleviate tension in the arms and hands.

The three most common grips are the ten finger grip, the Vardon grip, and the interlock grip. The ten finger grip, referred to by many as the baseball grip where all ten fingers are actually on the club, which is usually preferred by individuals with weaker hands.

There's the Vardon grip, also called the overlap grip.

This is a highly used method by many tour players. It is simply performed by taking the pinky finger of the rear hand, and placing it in the gap between the index and middle finger of the forward hand. The third grip, also widely used by some of the world's best players, is the interlock grip.

This is done by weaving the index finger of the forward hand between the pinky and next to pinky fingers of the rear hand. In general, one isn't better than the other, it's a matter of experimenting with each to see what works best for you. Each person has their own reason for favoring one over the other. Whichever grip you use though, it is real important to remember that the grip needs to be placed in the fingers and not buried in the palms. If you were going to throw a baseball, you wouldn't hold it in your palm, because you wouldn't get much action.

But if you hold it in the fingers, you could control it much better. That's where the sensory mechanism and feeling of control is.

Now, when placing the rear hand on the club, you need to place the club in the next to pinky and middle fingers.

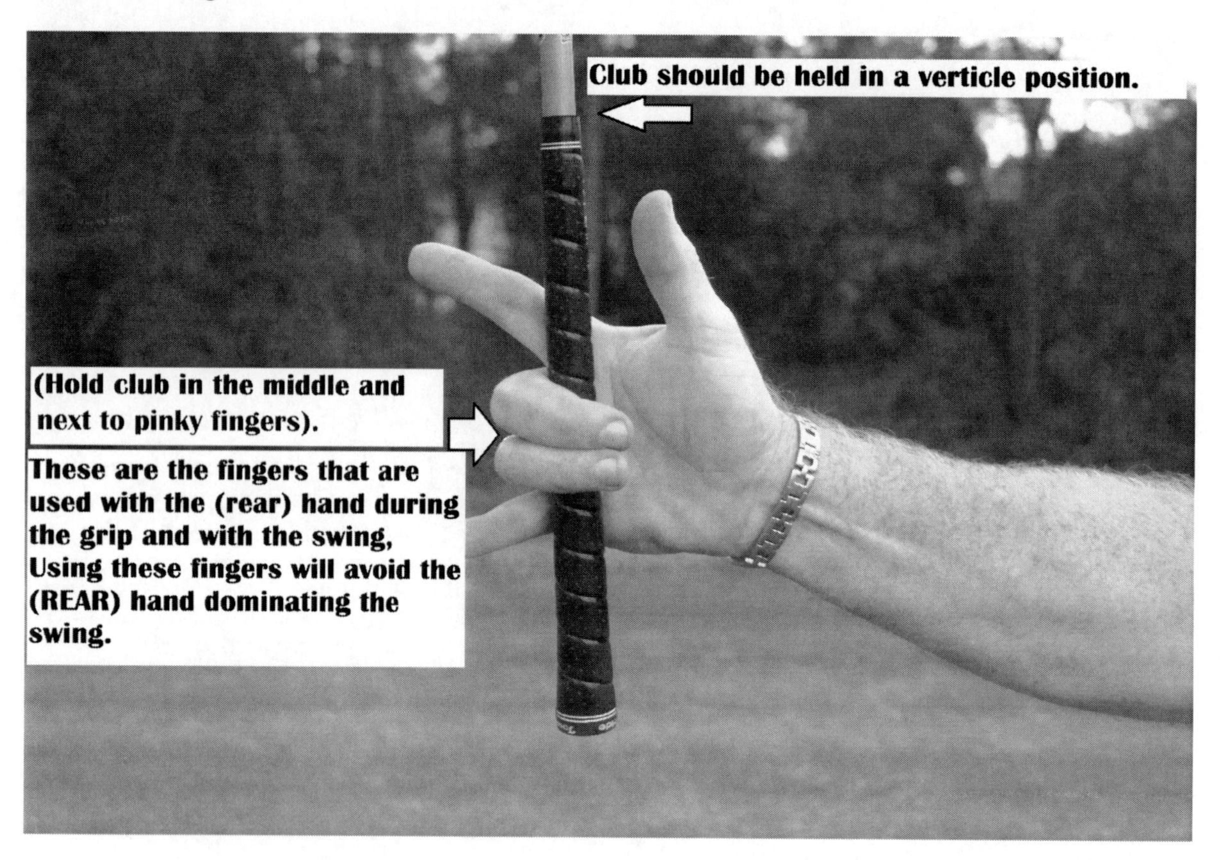

These are the main fingers used by the rear hand. You will want to avoid letting the rear hand become dominant in the swing and grip, which will lead to all kinds of problems, such as not properly releasing the club at impact. It also generates the feel that you want to choke the club and push with the rear hand, especially when you are really trying to hit the ball with a lot of force. This is among other things.

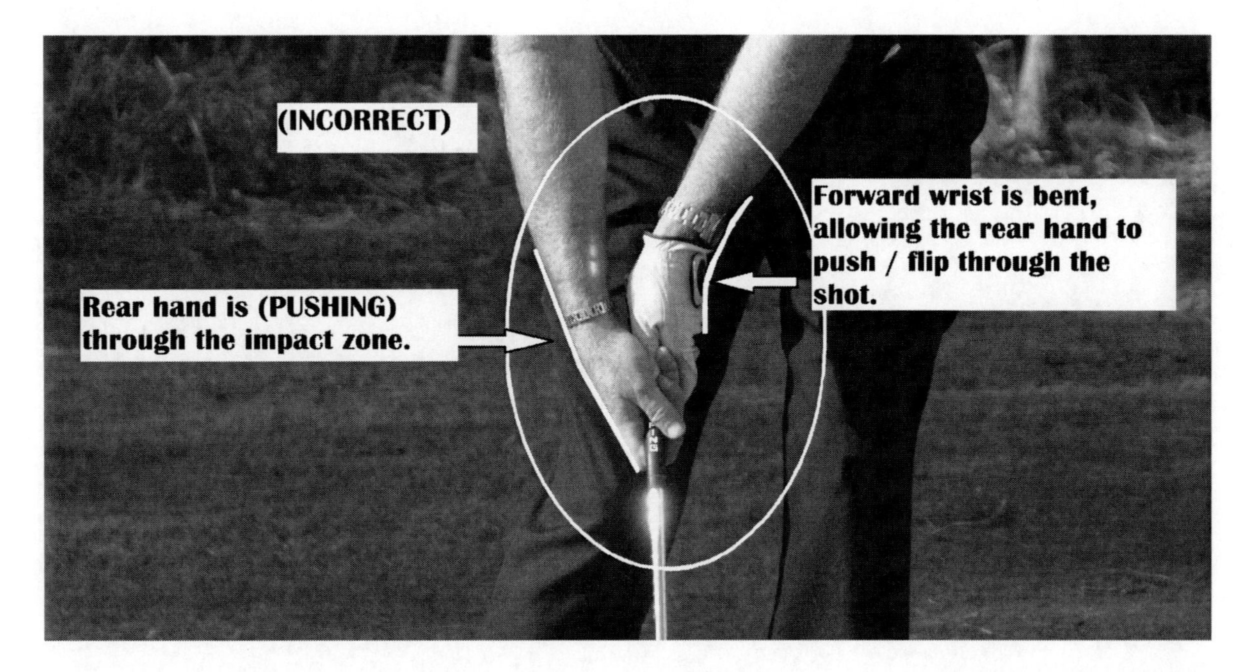

Now we usually use our favored hand for everything that we do like eating, throwing, writing, and so on. It's the hand we trust; so by nature, it will want to take over. In golf though, it needs to take a back seat and let the forward hand have a turn.

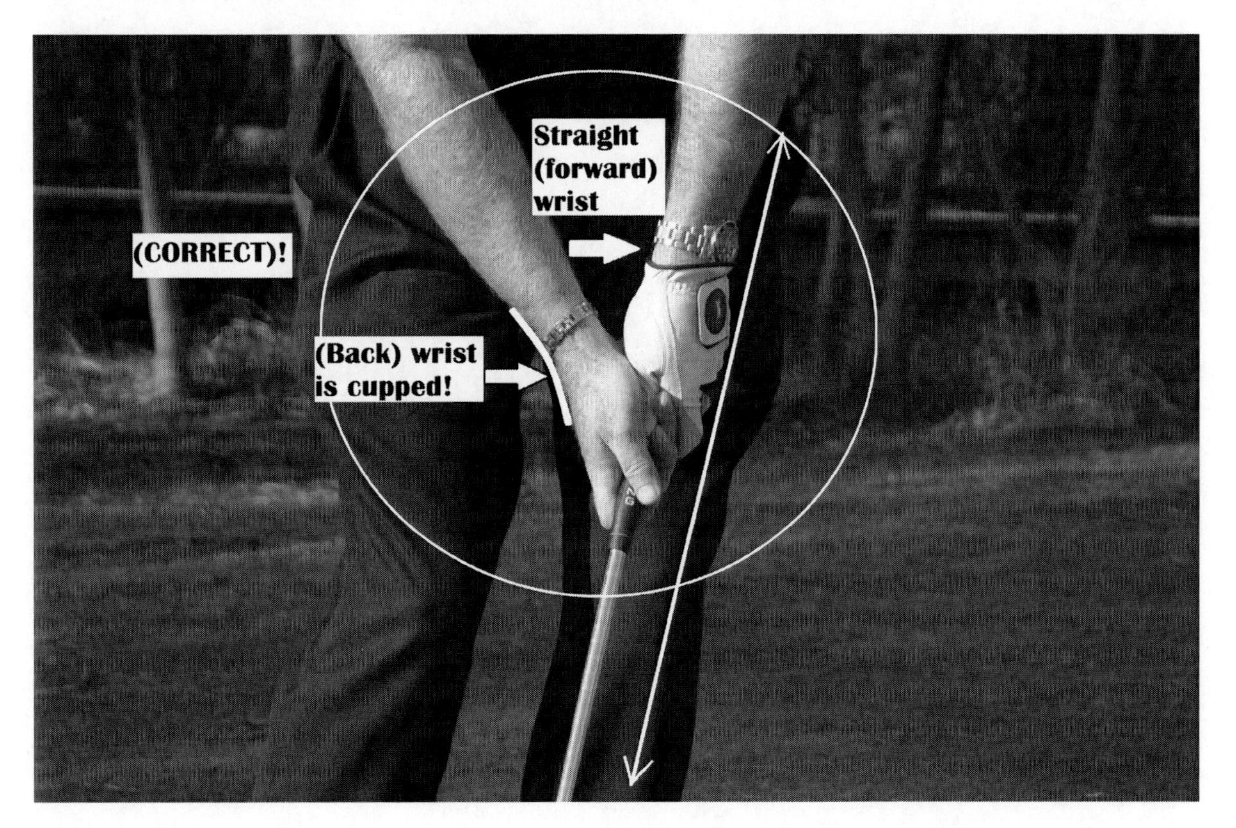

When your hands are on the club, at address, you'll want to ensure that they're working as one.

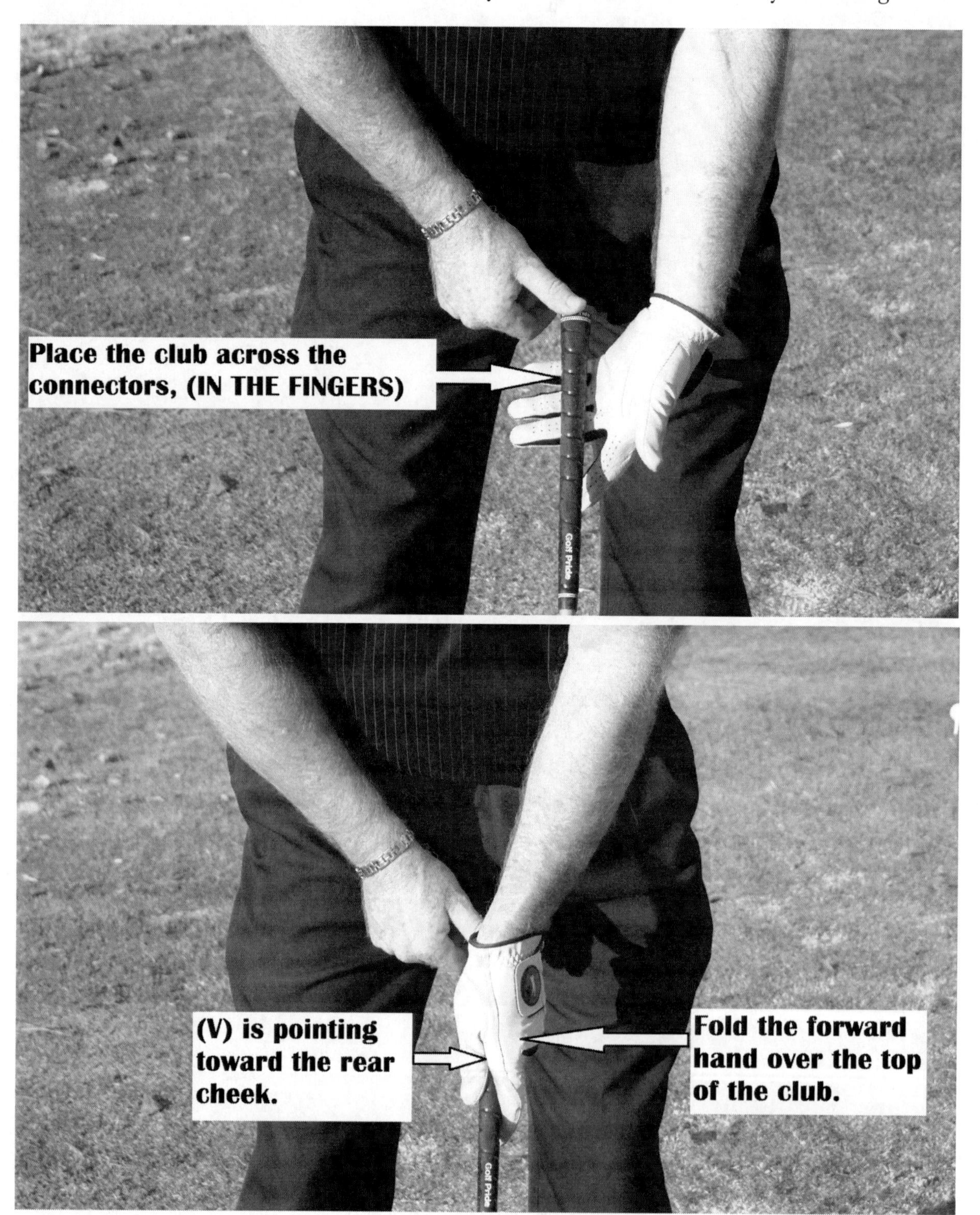

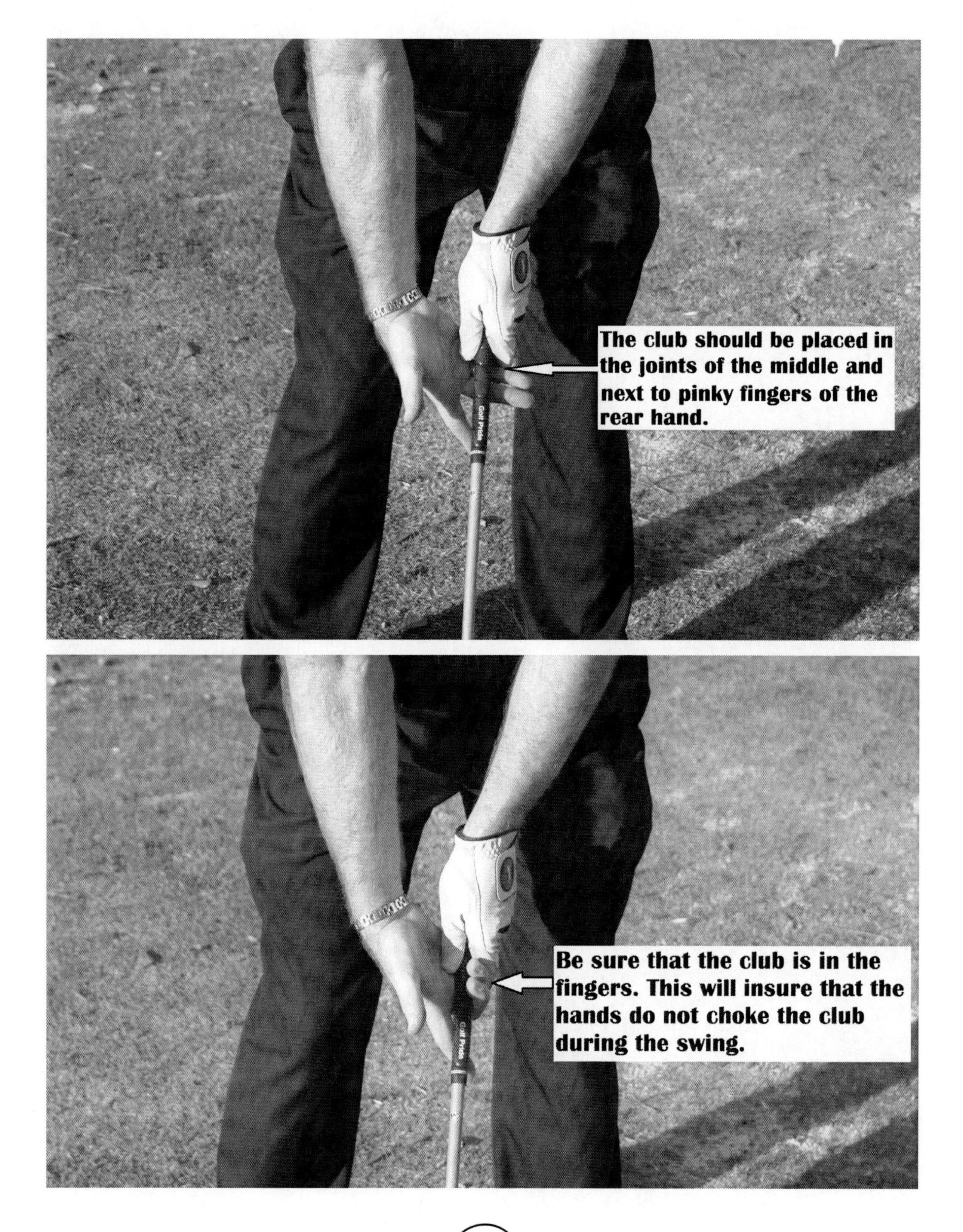
The club should be placed in the joints of the middle and next to pinky fingers of the rear hand.
Be sure that the club is in the fingers. This will insure that the hands do not choke the club during the swing.

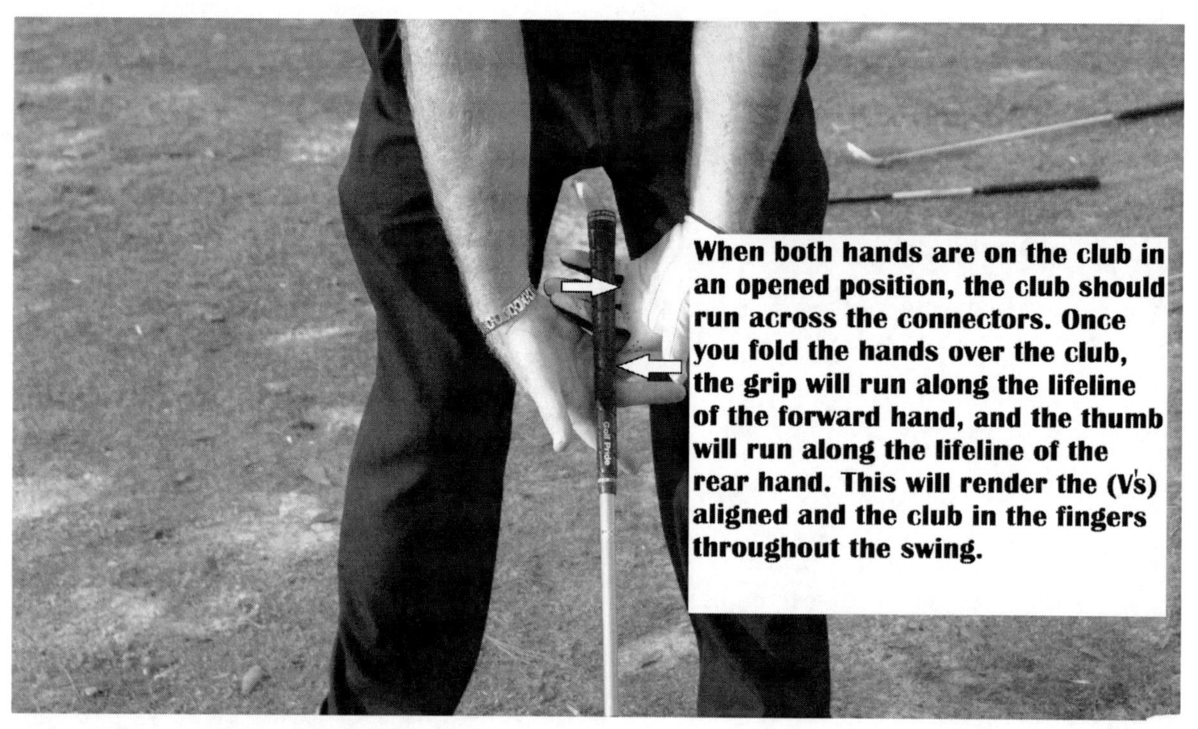

The V's should be aligned with each other and pointing toward the rear shoulder, which is an indication that your hands are aligned. The V's simply mean the area between the index finger and the thumb. It's very important that the V's be in a closed position and not gaping open. You can place two tees in them to check for alignment.

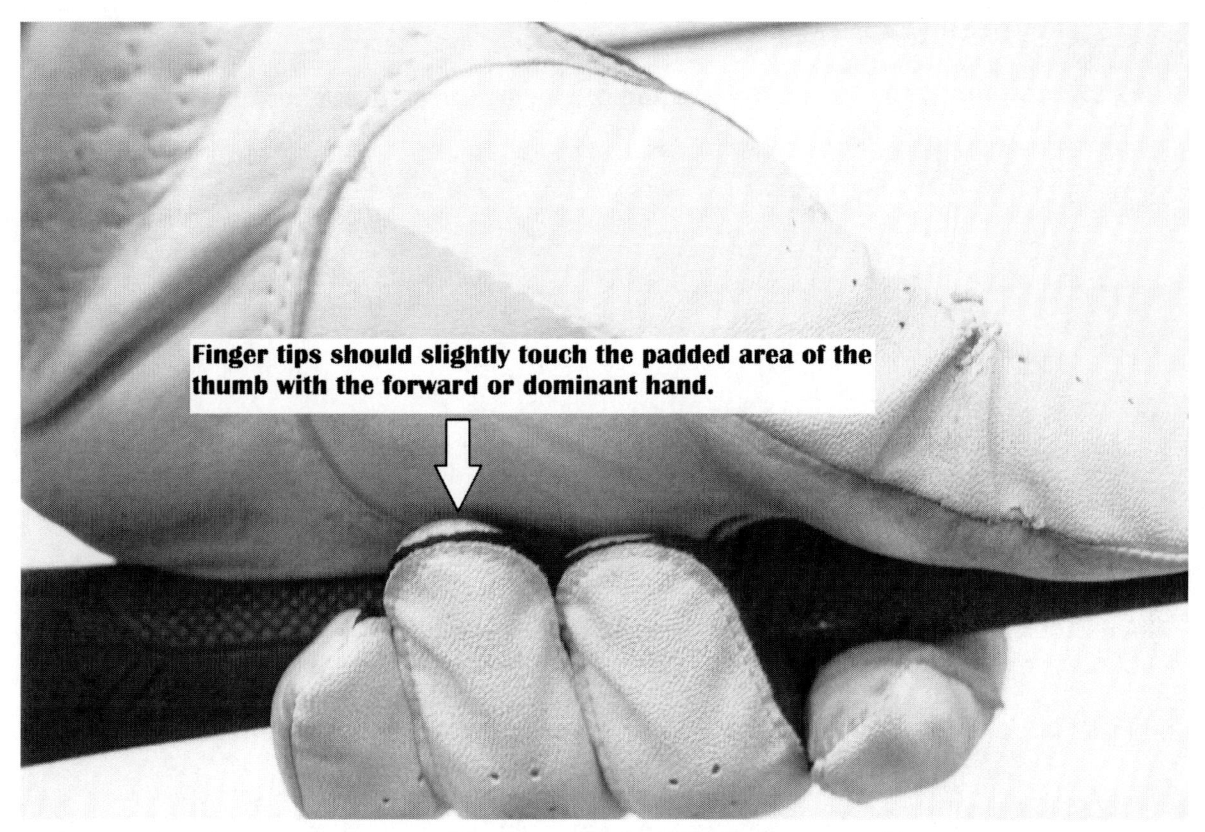

Remember that the alignment of your hands is extremely important. Try to imagine the hinges of a door. If the hinges are properly aligned, the door will open and close freely. However, if they're not aligned, you can still open the door, but it won't open as easily; and in time, the door casing will crack because the hinges are trying to go in two different directions. The hands work the same way. Imagine the tires on your vehicle. If the front end is out of alignment, you can still drive it; but it won't be long before it ruins the tires. Again, it's so important to have the hands aligned in the swing. This will allow a smooth release and ensure consistency in the shots, and the hands won't be fighting each other.

As we all know, there's thousands of training aids out there, which all seem to promise relief for your problems. If individuals really understood cause and effect as well as the correct body positions in the swing, they wouldn't become dependent on gadgets, and would be able to self correct. A lot of training aids come across as a quick fix, and end up being a crutch or a form of dependency. There are however, a few good ones that even tour pros use that do work. One item I highly recommend, especially for beginners, is something called a swing trainer.

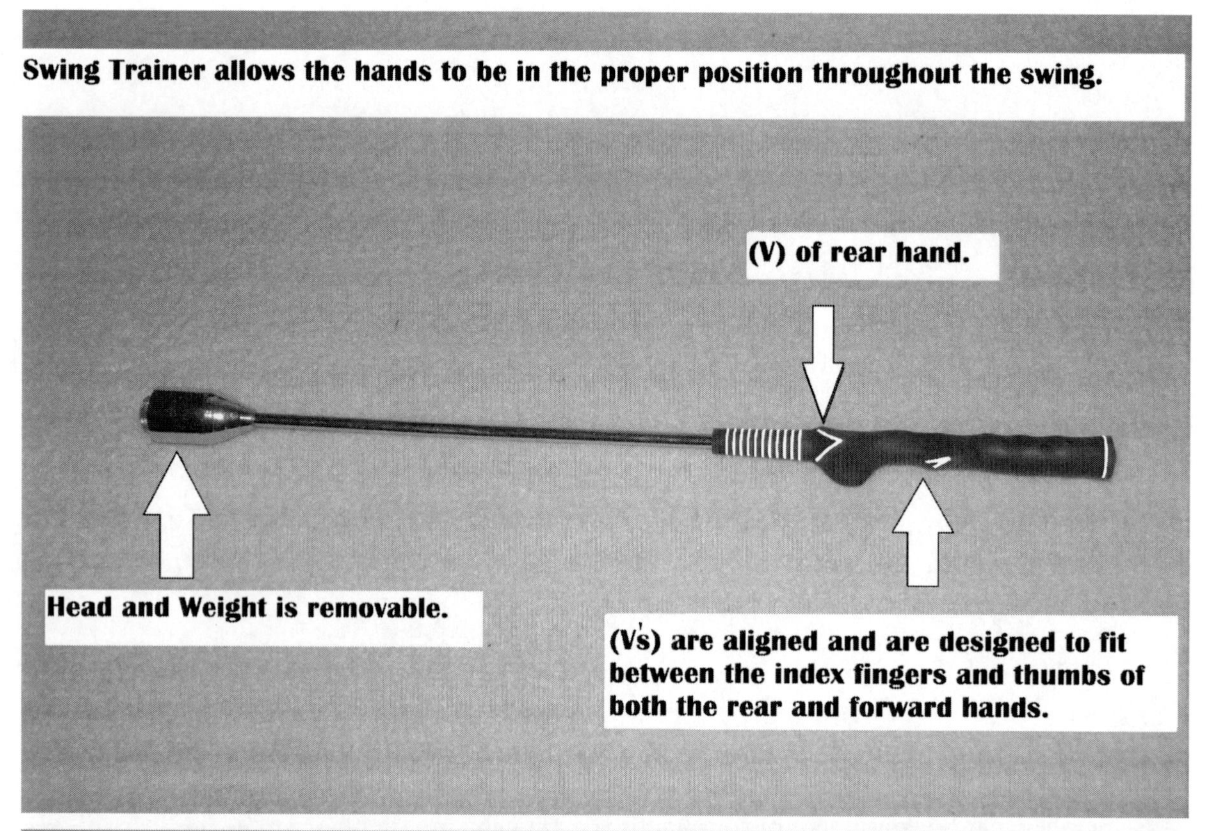

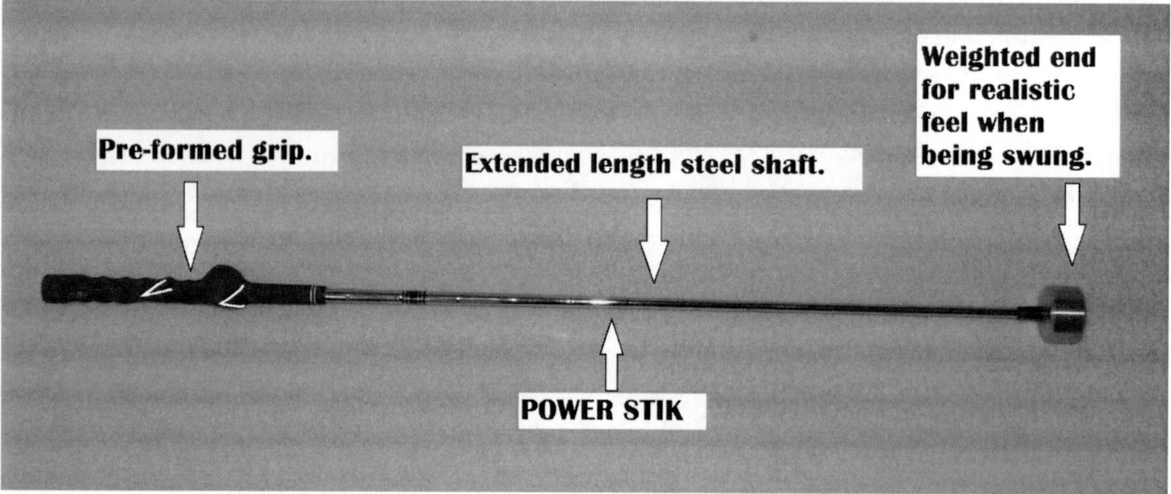

It has a pre-formed grip, which is ergonomically correct with the V's aligned, and it helps you with the feeling of correctness while actually making the swing. Now, I've been playing for many years; and still have it in my hands a few minutes each day. It's simply memorizing correctness.

POSTURE

I can't say enough about good posture. It's a very important part of the setup and should be maintained throughout the swing. Think of the framework of a house. Have you ever seen a house being built with just the frame exposed?

You can usually distinguish the shape just by looking at the framework. Your setup position is the same way. It's the infrastructure of the swing. When establishing your setup or posture, you're setting the foundation, finding a balanced position, and aligning the levers that will be used throughout the process. You'll either set yourself up for success or failure.

Understanding how the swing works is important, because it helps when setting the proper angles of the body. The first thing to remember is that the swing is produced with the core of the body and not the arms. I see so many people trying to swing with everything they have using only the arms and shoulders, and they wonder why they don't get much distance. In addition, you only set yourself up for injuries in the process.

When performing a correct swing, the arms merely take the energy produced by the body, and transfers it to the club as well as regulate the width of the swing.

That's the main role of the arms. It's like the transmission does in your vehicle. The horsepower actually comes from the engine and the transmission simply delivers it.

To start with, the feet need to be in a position that will support the movement of the body. It's important to have them in a position that will support the swing, but not too far apart. Something to keep in mind is, the farther your feet are from each other, the farther you have to travel when transferring your weight in the swing. So you don't want to be too spread out. Depending on the club being used, some being longer than others, the width will vary. If you were going to hit a driver, you would typically be in the widest position, probably just outside of the shoulders. However, if you were going to hit a wedge, you would have the feet much closer due to a tighter radius and less width in the swing. Now these are the two extremes, so the club and ball placement would vary somewhere in between.

A great tip to remember when placing your feet at address: to keep the rear foot perpendicular to the target line and turn the forward foot out just a little.

This will help alleviate unnecessary stress in the meniscus of the forward knee and make it easier to finish the swing.

One of the first things that most people notice is the main core of the body or the spine angle. It's important to have the back as straight as possible, because the turn of the body in the swing is basically around the spine, sometimes called a fixed axis. However, I prefer to use the term center, or core axis, due to the fact that the spine isn't really fixed. It represents a center point of reference. There are countless body types, and people are built differently; and flexibility will have a huge effect on the ability to perform certain positions as well. Keep in mind though, the straighter your back, the easier it is to make things happen correctly.

The easiest way to ensure your back is straight during the swing is to simply take a club from your bag, place it behind you while standing straight up, it should maintain contact with your lower, middle, and upper back, as well as the back of your head.

From there, bend at the hips and try to maintain contact with all four points.

If your back isn't straight, you will lose contact at one of the two ends. This will make you aware of whether your back is straight or not. From there, simply hold the position, and bring the club over the shoulder and down into the hitting position.

You can also take the club and place it along the front of the shoulders at the very top so it has equal distance hanging out over each side and rotate in both directions.

Try to touch a point of reference at both ends.

You can use a doorknob or something stationary to gage the rotation. This will show how the body rotates in the swing while maintaining the spine angle. It also ensures that the body isn't tilting. Try to make sure that the center of the chest touches the club as well. This will let you know if you're allowing the shoulders to round out. The legs should be slightly flexed or bent, and not locked. This allows for balance and fluid movement.

The knees should be forward or toward the toes, which will vary depending on how much the legs are flexed or bent. Try to have your rear end acting as a counterbalance hanging about an inch or so behind the heels. Your weight should be centered over the forward part of the arches of the feet.

Now some teachers say that all of the weight should be on the balls of the feet where others see it differently. I've found that balancing the use of the quads (*forward leg muscles*) and hamstrings (*back muscles*) will help maximize the use and conservation of energy and place the center of gravity over the forward portion of the arches. I suggest that you experiment for yourself and see what works best for you.

In golf, you will commonly hear the phrase "down the line" view. A down the line view is similar to what a baseball catcher would see looking back at the pitcher.

It's an imaginary straight line from the ball to the target. From this view, one is able to observe the alignment as well as body angles of the person hitting. Depending on the club being used, the arms are going to hang at different angles. This is because the length of the club and the swing plane will vary. For example, if you were going to hit a driver, your arms would be farther away from the body, due to the fact that the club is longer. Whereas, if you were hitting a wedge or 9 iron shot, the hands would be much closer to the body. In general with the irons, the forward hand should be about one hand width from the zipper to the butt of the club.

I see a lot of players addressing the ball with it too far away. These are usually individuals that are carrying a few extra pounds. They feel as though they need the extra room to get around and through the shot.

Teeing too far away causes a lot of problems. The center of gravity and balance is affected the farther you are from the center.

If something is thrown at your eyes you'll blink without thinking about it, this is a mechanism that is built into us. Balance works the same way. The body automatically recovers its balance without you realizing it. If you recall ever hitting your foot, stumbling, or tripping on something, you would automatically step out to recover. Standing up in the swing is basically the same thing. As a result, this will usually lead to topping the ball, hitting a fat shot, whiffing the shot, swinging across the line or hitting off the toe of the club. It also inhibits the ability to transfer the weight in the right direction.

The easiest way to find the optimal address position is to imagine an athletic stance. Think back to when we used to play a game called Burnout.

This is an athletic position which is the same as the address position.

This is where two people would throw a baseball as hard as they could to each other attempting to get the other person to drop it. Now you have no idea if the other person could throw well or not; so you would need to be in a balanced and ready position that would allow you to move in any direction. With this thought in mind, the address position is the same. This should be the same balanced position as your address, ready to put the body into motion while remaining balanced. As you're starting to see, good posture does play a big role throughout the swing. It's the beginning of the swing; and since it's non-moving, you can get it right every time.

You've probably heard people tell you all of your life to "keep your head down!" What you need to understand, is this phrase is relative. Down is where the chin is practically on the chest.

If your head is in that position, how can you properly rotate your shoulders? The head should actually be up, which really means, the back of the head needs to remain consistent with the spine angle.

What you don't want to do is lift your head to see where the ball went; in general that's what they are referring to. Although, the head doesn't stay perfectly still in the swing, it needs to stay steady. Remember, movement of the head going up and down is usually an indication of body movement. This will ensure that the body and shoulders are properly rotating.

Now that the body angles are established, everything is set into position to perform what's known as a swing plane. In golf, a swing plane is defined as the path that the arms, hands, and club travel around an axis, represented as the spine.

If you put an object on the end of a string and twirl it around, you will see that there is an established plane. It can be straight or tilted. It really doesn't matter, there's still a swing plane. This is true with the clubhead going around the body. It's only connected by the arms, hands, and the shaft of the club. Ultimately, if you think about it, the ball just gets in the way of the clubface. The swing plane is very important, because it ultimately dictates the direction and rotation of the club throughout the swing relative to the body.

You'll commonly hear of the player's swing being on plane, above plane, or flat which is below the vertical plane. These are vital during the backswing. There are certain characteristics that go with each type of swing. The simplest way to think of it is if there were an imaginary piece of plywood that is tilted with a hole cut in it that you place the upper body in—from the armpits up, from underneath. Going from the address position, the club and hands would simply travel up the board, then back down the board through impact, and back up the other side. This is a simple version of the swing plane. In the actual swing though, in a down the line view, the club should travel slightly outside the hands on the way up, then more inside on the way down.

This is because you're trying to get the swing as wide as possible on the way up; then from the top of the swing, the club should fall into what is referred to as the slot. This will bring it a little farther inside on the way down.

Now, the reason this happens is simply because the body is compressing on the back side. Remember, the swing is accumulating torque and tension because of the turning of the body. The lower half is resisting, and the upper half is coiling. This resistance, or torque, is what will be released in the swing to deliver the energy into the ball through impact. The back side of the body drops, and becomes much closer to the rear hip as the hips rotate. This intensifies the energy going through the shot. At the same time, the forward side is stretching. As the hips rotate, along with the core of the body, the angles direct the energy through the arms, the club, and ultimately into the ball. Now this is where what is commonly referred to as the angle or lag comes into play. What they're referring to is the angle established between the forward arm and the shaft of the club.

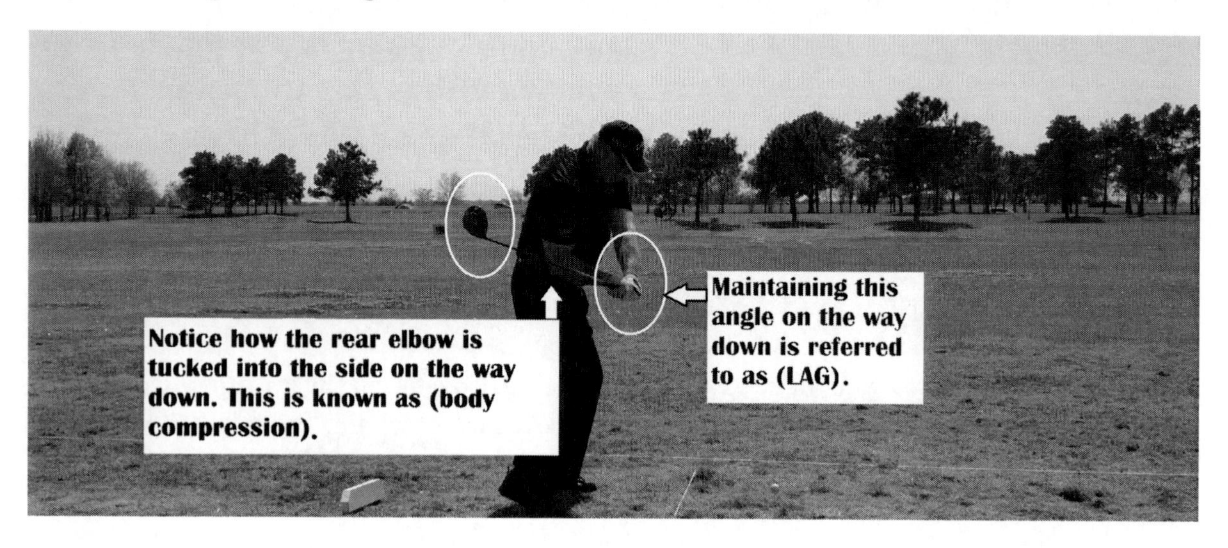

If you think of a bullwhip, picture just taking it and swinging it over your head toward your target; basically, it would just make a swishing sound and travel at the same speed throughout the motion. Now if you hold an angle in the wrist and then let it go during the swing, you will release the energy down the whip and you'll get it to pop. And of course, the end of the whip would be traveling much faster. We do the same thing with the club. The idea is to time the release of the club in the impact zone, also referred to as the *moment of truth*.

While watching advanced players on TV, it appears they swing relatively easy, yet it goes so far. They've refined their swing to make this happen. Remember, contrary to popular belief, power has nothing to do with brute strength; it's all about proper application.

BALL POSITION

There are two things to consider when determining ball position. First, how far it should be placed from the body, and second, is how far forward or back it should be in the stance. Distance from the body will be determined by the length of the club and the posture of the person hitting. Once good posture is established, distance is relatively easy to acquire. In the chapter about posture, I spoke about teeing the ball too far away and how it creates difficulty in maintaining balance while in motion. The second problem though—especially with the irons—is if the club is too far away from the body, it will tend to be too flat with the lie angle, which means the heel is lower than the toe. This will lead to inconsistent shots. At impact, the heel will dig and the toe will flip over, so you can see where this could be a problem. The easiest way to see if this is happening is to stand in front of a mirror sideways, look at your posture, and look at the bottom edge of the club.

The center of the bottom edge or flange should be touching the ground. Adjust the distance in either direction to find the center of the flange. You can also check your divots, they will provide valuable information.

I have students always asking me, "What is the perfect ball position?" The truth is, there is no set answer. Optimal ball position will continually changed based on many variables such as, their particular swing, the club, the shot they're trying to make, the lie of the ball, and the loft of the club, etc.

For instance, if you're hitting a driver, you'd want to play the ball more forward;

because with a driver, you want to hit the ball in a level or slightly upward motion. This is due to the fact that, with an upward motion, there will be much less spin resulting in greater distance. Whereas, the irons would be hit in a downward direction or descending blow, which results in what is referred to as compressing the ball. In this situation you'd probably want to play the ball a little farther back.

With the irons it is important that the bottom of the swing, which is called the apex, be in front of the ball. This is the part of the swing where the clubface reaches its lowest point before starting to rise again.

With the irons, the (APEX) lowest point of the swing should be about 4" beyond the ball. This results in ball compression.

This is what causes the divot in the ground, which should always be beyond the ball. The divot or dig doesn't affect the flight of the ball, it's just an indication that the ball was struck in a downward motion. This is how you control the flight of the ball, known as working the ball.

Ball position is something individuals should experiment with. If someone doesn't get much exercise, chances are they don't have much flexibility, and might find it easier to play the ball a little farther back in their stance; whereas, someone in relatively good shape may be able to get more forward in the shot so they would probably benefit by playing it a little farther up. If you are on uneven ground, high grass, chipping, or needing to avoid an obstacle, this would dictate the ball position as well. It's a great idea to practice all of these scenarios so that when you find yourself challenged with them, you'll know what works best. I'll be covering some of these situations in detail further in the book.

One of the first questions I always ask when interviewing a new student is whether or not they take a divot with their irons. I can usually anticipate their answer based on their reaction. A lot of them will roll their eyes up as though they were accessing a memory, then reply, "Well, sometimes!" The truth is, if it's not an immediate yes, then the answer is no. I always emphasize the importance of taking a divot with an iron. This is extremely important, because compressing the ball greatly affects ball flight and placement. If you look at the bottom or flange of an iron, you'll see that they're rounded on the bottom.

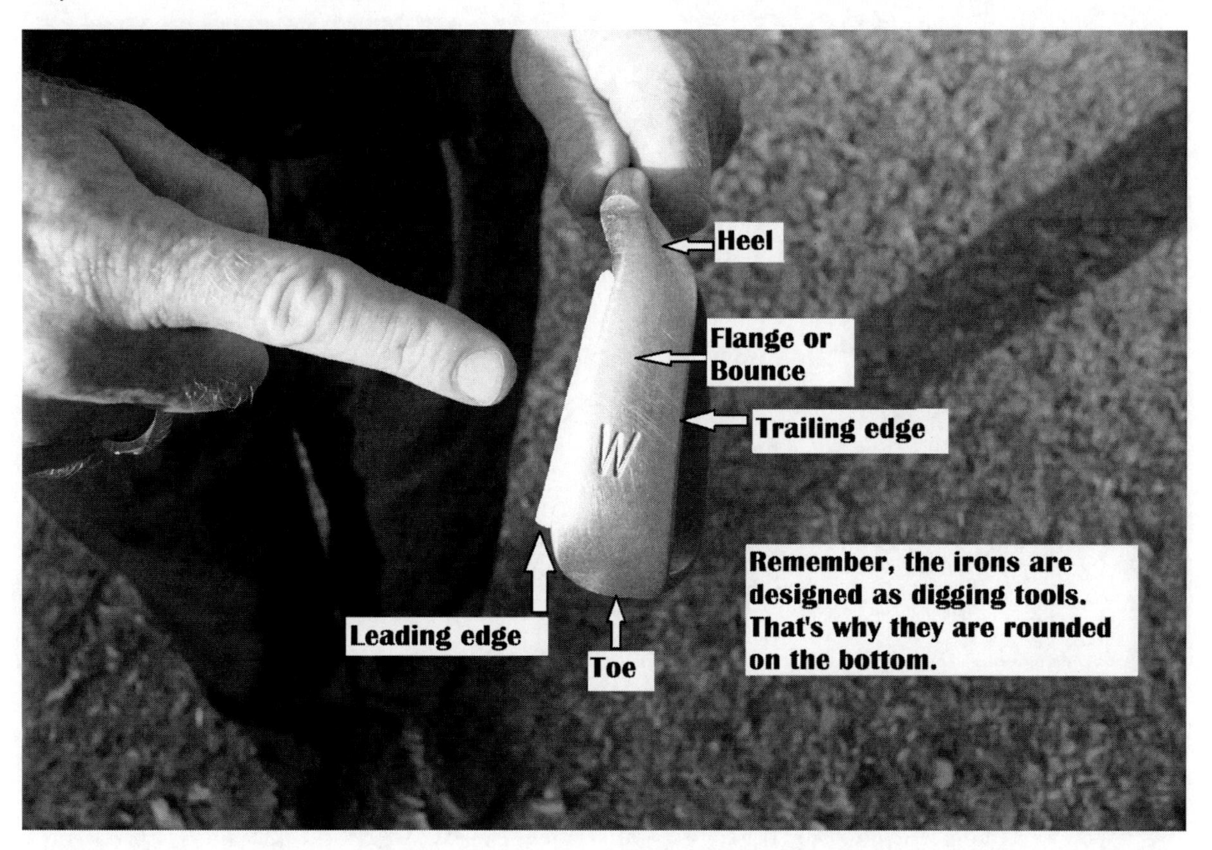

The irons are actually designed as digging tools. In general though, people tend to avoid hitting the ground, trying to protect their club, their hands, and even the ground itself. They try to scoop or spoon the ball and cleanly pick it off the ground by helping it into the air. With the exception of the flop shot, nothing could be more wrong.

Inexperienced players tend to sweep the ball cleanly off the ground and try to help it into the air. However, against our natural instincts, it is important to hit down onto the ball. This allows the club to do what it was designed to do. During the impact with the face of the club; and the ball, several things come into play. While the shaft of the club is pointing straight up, descending into the ball, there is very little clubface surface coming into contact with it.

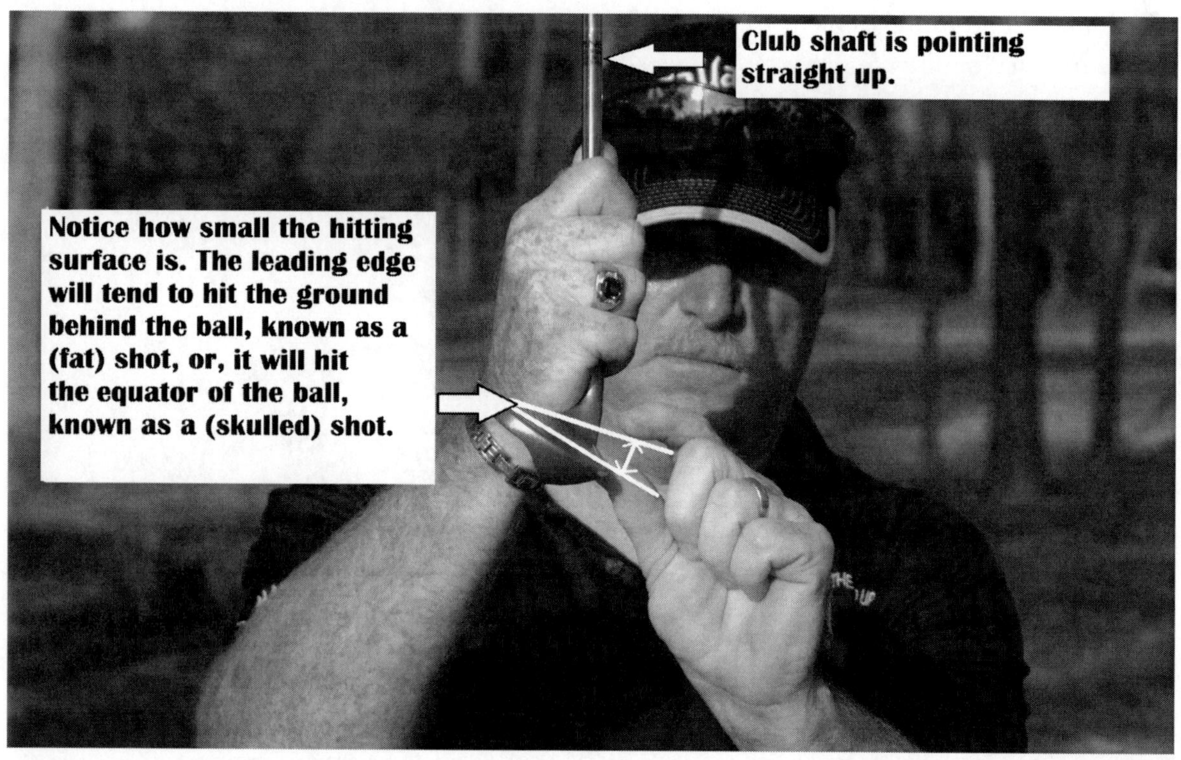

This leaves little margin for error, which significantly reduces the striking area. This will result in skulling the ball or hitting it fat, which means hitting the ground behind the ball. However, by leaning the shaft of the club forward and hitting down onto the ball,

the face becomes much larger with an increased hitting area.

Here's something else. I want you to imagine taking a golf ball, and throwing it against a concrete wall. If it is thrown at a forty-five degree angle, it will bounce off of the wall, experiencing a certain amount of compression as it ricochets. But if you throw it directly at the wall, it will bounce harder and compress more due to a blunt strike, which equates to additional yards. Additionally, compressing the ball harder brings the grooves more into play. Think of your fingernails digging into a baseball or sandpaper on your fingertips. You would get more traction on the surface of the ball.

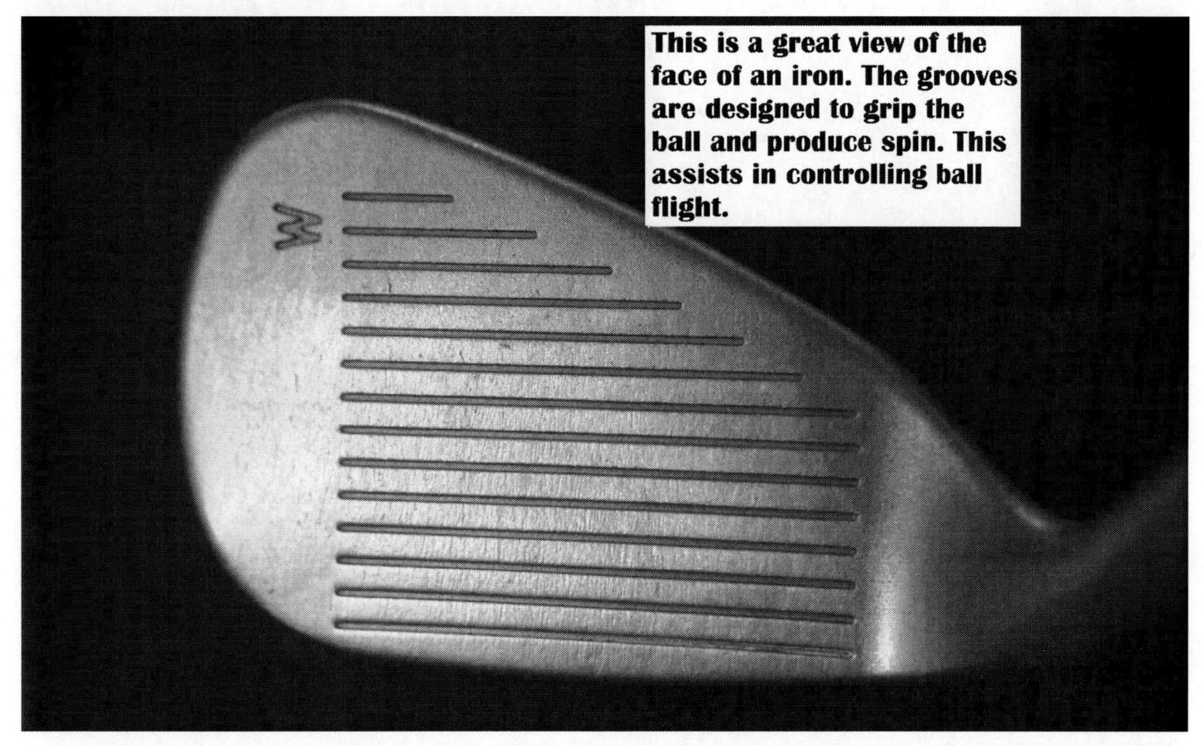

This is a great view of the face of an iron. The grooves are designed to grip the ball and produce spin. This assists in controlling ball flight.

Something else to consider when you try to pick the ball cleanly off the ground is: you're vulnerable to the conditions of the course. Whether you're playing on a hard surface or in high grass, you'll know what I'm talking about. Remember, you won't always have a clean, nice, and fluffy or perched lie. But if you hit down on the ball and take a divot, it doesn't matter so much about the ground because you strike the ball, the ball rockets off the face, and then you take a divot. This takes the ground out of the equation.

There are other reasons to move the ball around as well. When playing in very windy conditions, you would want to play what's known as a *knockdown shot*, which simply means hitting the ball at a lower trajectory and eliminating the effect of the wind. This is also a shot you would probably consider when needing to go under an object such as a tree; or if you miss the fairway and just want to get it back in play.

So you can see there are a variety of reasons to move the ball around for different shots. This is something you should spend time practicing and experimenting with; allowing you to see what each shot will produce. They all have a time and purpose, and it's great to have the shot in your bag when needed. For normal shots with a short to mid-iron, I tend to play the ball in the center of my stance; and with the longer irons, I'll tend to play the ball progressively forward. It's important to remember though, ball movement should be kept to a minimum, because excessive ball movement can affect alignment. Again, this is an individual thing, depending on how much movement you make in your swing. You'll need to take the time to find which one works best for you. When you're warming up, take a few relaxed swings, not aiming at any particular point and strike the ground. It will help identify the best and most natural place to put the ball. Depending on how you might feel that day, ball position may change a little.

ALIGNMENT

Alignment is very important because a great shot is no good unless it goes in the right direction, and travels to the intended target. This is also extremely important because it's the part of the swing that sets the pace for the rest of the shot. You practice hitting balls to promote consistency in your shots. Remember, you don't change your swing to fit the direction. If you're sighting the scope of a rifle, you don't take the scope off and remount it when you miss the target, and then try again. You simply make adjustments to the existing position. The swing is the same way. Once you align certain parts of the body in your setup—being the feet, knees, hips, shoulders, and even the eyes

the direction of the ball should be the same provided you swing along the body line. Now a lot of people worry about foot alignment. The truth is, that's not as important as the four other key points.

The ones you need to really focus on are knees, hips, shoulders, and eyes; with the shoulders being the most important. The alignment with the eyes is simply a proper turning of the head and not the body. It helps to just think of looking under the shot. Remember, the imaginary shaft goes from the sky, through the neck and down the back. The turning of the head should be along this axis.

You can place two rods on the ground in a parallel position in the direction of the target to assist in body alignment.

These rods can be found in many hardware stores. Some players just use one or two clubs, anything straight will work. What these two lines represent is close to body alignment and ball path alignment. They're like railroad tracks. This is great to practice with in training your eyes as well as your swing. It promotes consistency and gives you feedback when you veer from your target. After years of playing, I was in a practice round, and another player standing behind me asked why I was in an opened position. For a right-handed player, that simply means that the body is aligned slightly to the left. I had triple checked myself, and I was convinced that I was square to the target line. He placed a club at my toes in the direction I was pointing, I stepped behind the shot and sure enough, I was indeed opened to the line. Now what that revealed to me is my perception was distorted. I got so used to looking at what I thought was correct that I believed it was. That happens to golfers all the time. It was then that I realized no matter what your skill level is, you will always benefit from this.

BALL FLIGHT

When hitting a golf ball, impact will always produce a spin. Spin is the result of the face angle at impact and the direction the club is traveling, known as the swing path. One is relative to the other, and together they will always produce a spin. You can use a Ping-Pong paddle and ball to test this. It works great because the reaction is more obvious with a Ping-Pong ball due to its characteristics. If the direction of your swing path is in-to-out, and the face is square to the target line, the ball will have a spin and produce a curved ball flight in one direction. Just the opposite, out-to-in will produce the opposite flight.

This is due to something known as the *Magnus effect (force)*. When a spherical object is sent into motion, it will have spin on it. As it travels through the atmosphere, one side of the object will be traveling faster than the other due to the fact one side is in the return direction, which is caused by rotation.

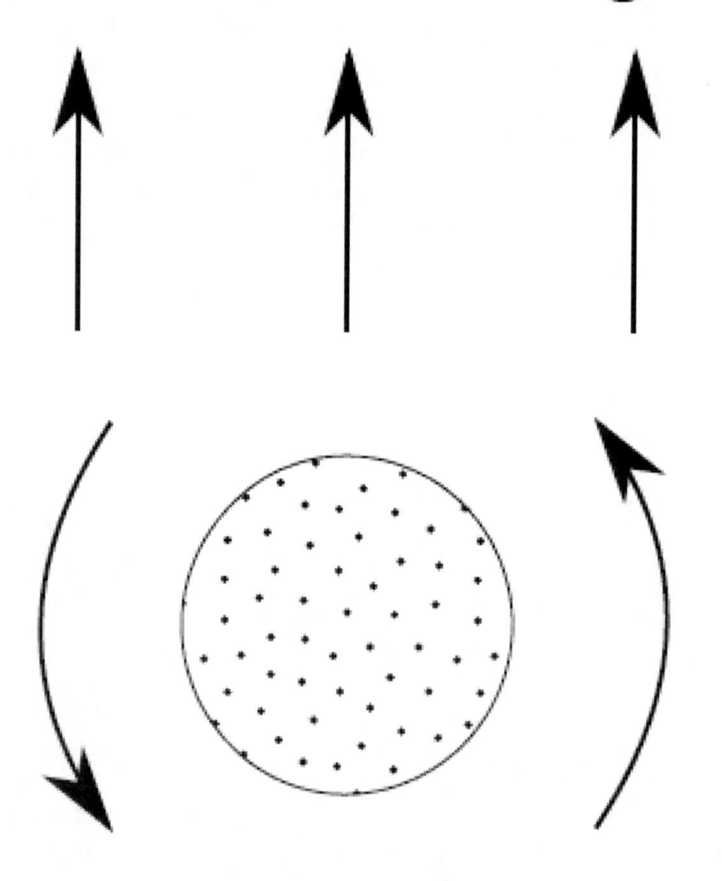

This creates a difference in air pressure on one side of the ball verses the other while in flight. The faster the ball is moving, the greater the force; thus, bending the path of the object. That's why in baseball, the pitcher exerts a lot of spin on the ball to curve it. This same effect is applied onto the golf ball when working it around objects and manipulating the flight of the ball. When deciding which choice to make, you need to consider these facts.

When a right-handed player hits a draw shot, right to left it will produce a lower ball flight and tend to roll more after it lands.

This happens because the face of the club is de-lofted and slightly closed relative to the swing path. Whereas, a fade or left to right shot, also referred to as a cut shot, will usually produce a higher ball flight and land softer; because the face would be more lofted and opened relative to the swing path. It also tends to spend more time in the air and won't roll as far when it lands.

There are certain factors that come into play, that favor one option over another. For instance, on a windy or dry day, you'd want to keep the shot lower and out of the wind, so a draw might be ideal for these conditions. On a day when the ground is soft, wet, or if you're hitting onto an island green, you'd want as much air time as possible; because once it lands, it won't roll much. The fade shot might be a better option. The correct way to produce this shot is actually quite simple. When addressing the ball have the leading edge of the clubface point directly at the target, then take an open stance relative to the target.

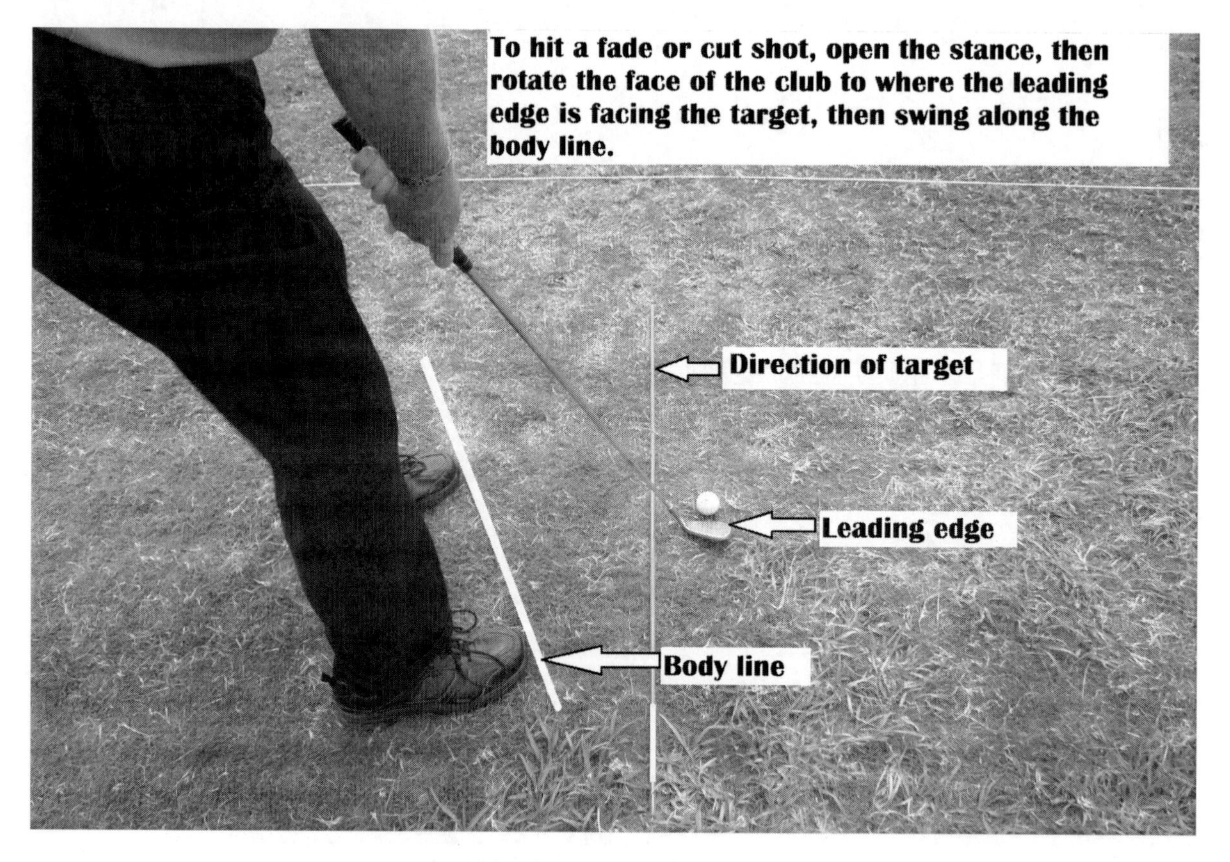

Then take a normal swing along your body line. This will produce the shot. The farther you turn, the more the ball will move or curve. Just the opposite, when hitting a draw, turn the other way or take a closed stance, square the clubface to the target and make your swing along the body line.

This is a (closed) address position. Leading edge is facing the target. To hit a draw shot, take a normal swing along the body line. This will produce the correct spin on the ball.
Direction of target
Leading edge
Body alignment
Ball flight
Alignment
Swing path
Square to target
Club direction

This will produce the desired ball flight.

Something to be aware of—when you're directing or aiming the clubface to an object or target—it is important to use the leading edge, which is located at the bottom of the clubface. There are some instructors that believe in using the center or even the top of the clubhead. Depending on the particular clubs, this could be misleading. If your clubs are *offset* at all, it will tend to throw you off. This is something that you will need to spend time practicing once you get comfortable with these shots; I am certain that you will find them very useful. It will certainly create more versatility in your shot arsenal. Understanding the laws of ball flight is very important. There are nine possible shots that can be made. *See the following diagram.*

BALL FLIGHT LAWS

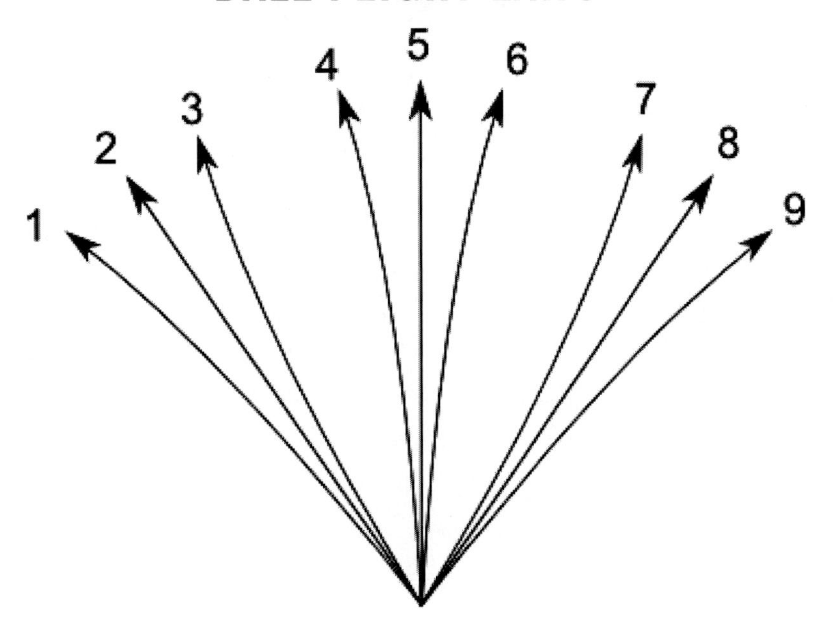

In this diagram, you will see nine possible ball flights, which are numbered. Use the lines to identify each ball flight corresponding with the common verbiage in golf.

Right Handed		Left Handed
(1)	PULL HOOK	(9)
(2)	PULLED SHOT	(8)
(3)	PULL SLICE	(7)
(4)	HOOKED SHOT	(6)
(5)	STRAIGHT SHOT	(5)
(6)	SLICED SHOT	(4)
(7)	PUSH HOOK	(3)
(8)	PUSH SHOT	(2)
(9)	PUSH SLICE	(1)

The flight of the ball is determined by the path of the clubhead at impact and the clubface angle relative to the path. When striking the ball, the combination of the two will produce spin and direction on the ball, which ultimately influences the path that the ball with travel. Accomplished players will actually use different flight lines to accommodate certain shots, manipulating the flight of the ball, curving around objects, as well as regulating the loft.

WEIGHT DISTRIBUTION

Two things that are exceptionally important throughout the swing are, where your weight is, and which direction it is moving. Proper balance is needed in order to transfer weight at any given time to the correct position. The main objective is to keep your weight confined to the area between the inside edges of your feet, ensuring that it moves in the direction of the swing.

Starting in the address position your weight should be evenly distributed between both feet.

As you start the takeaway, your weight should begin transferring to the rear foot and continue to the top of the backswing. It is very important that you not let your weight exceed the inside of the rear foot.

For example, if you were going to throw a baseball, you would limit the back of the wind-up to where you could quickly change directions and stride toward the target. However, if you go too far back, you will get hung up and not be able to change directions. The swing is the same way. The easiest way to perform this is to ensure that the top button of your shirt stays inside the rear foot at the top of your swing.

When hitting your irons, think of cranking a lawn mower.

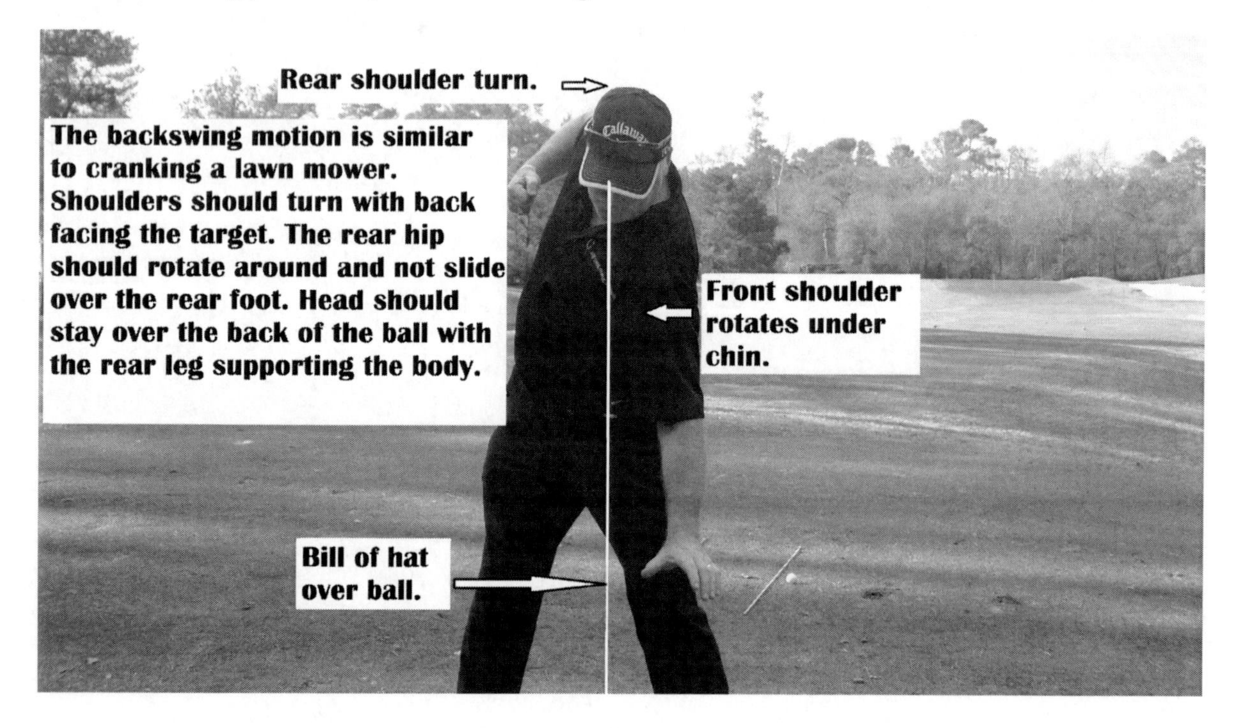

Your head stays steady and your weight basically loads into the rear hip. This will give you a slightly forward spine angle while correctly turning your shoulders and pointing your back to the target. It sets you up for a forward thrust, making it easier to shift your weight forward. With the driver, you will want to keep your head behind the ball at impact, due to an ascending blow, so your weight should transition through the mid-section and hips.

Remember, the club is being held by the arms, which are connected to the upper body. This will help you stay farther back and still transfer your weight aggressively. Something that will assist you in transferring your weight forward in the downswing is to get a wedge, golf ball, or even a book; place it under the outside edge of your back foot and practice hitting balls.

This will give you the feeling of weight transfer from the top of your backswing in the direction of the target. At the finish of your swing all of your weight should be on the front foot. Two things to keep in mind, at the completion of your swing you should be able to lift your rear foot without losing balance and your forward foot should be in the original address position, which is slightly turned out. If your forward foot spins and points toward the target, this is an indication your weight was on the heels.

PRE-SHOT ROUTINE

This is the point in time when you gather relevant information, analyze your options, develop a strategy, such as the ball flight, if the wind will affect your shot, if there are any hazards, and the desired landing area; well, you get the idea. Some players find it beneficial to visual the shot prior to actually taking it. Once you have gathered the information you need, now is the time to determine your shot and commit to it.

This includes things on your personal checklist as well, such as remembering to keep a steady head, don't flip the hands, weight transfer, or anything you struggle with, etc. The purpose of a pre-shot routine is like that of a pilot. He could easily jump into the cockpit, fire up the aircraft engines, and take off. Instead, he methodically goes through a checklist, this way he will leave with confidence knowing everything is as it should be. This is the same mind-set as the pre-shot routine, taking the information in and committing to the shot. The pre-shot routine is something you need to do on the practice tee as well. The practice range is where habits are formed, good or bad. Make a habit of thinking through your shot before you step into the hitting area, this is imperative and should be done every single time. This is also the point in time where you are aligning your shot. Now remember, with every golf shot, you need to do three things—evaluate the situation, determine your options, and then choose the shot that you are most comfortable with.

How many times have you heard or even said yourself, "I was hitting them so well on the range, but now I can't get anything to work!" Gee, what happened? That's more common than people realize. What they don't understand is that they have actually learned two different games. When they are on the range, they are hitting one shot after another at a rapid pace. They never step away from the address position to consider the whole shot.

Spend time giving thought to each shot when practicing. Remember, time spent on the range is a rehearsal for what you will do while on the golf course. Establish a PRE-SHOT routine. This is where habits are formed.

They have no thought process, and just hit away with no goal in mind. When they get on the course, they realize that every shot counts, then they feel lost. The idea behind the pre-shot routine is to gather all of your thoughts, consider your options, recognize your challenges, and commit to your shot. Most important though, this needs to become a habit. It becomes a comfort zone; and when you're on the course, it becomes something that you have rehearsed and are familiar with. What I'm going to do is take you through my routine and thought process.

If you watch much golf, you'll notice that the pros stand behind the ball. It's important to realize, what they are doing is actually separating the routine into two segments. Behind the ball is what we call the *think box;*

and where the feet are placed in the address position is referred to as the *execution box*. The first part of the pre-shot routine is performed in the think box. This is where we gather information to determine our options such as a favorable landing area, where the ball will come to rest, and elements that may affect our shot. It is very important to be completely confident with your club selection and your shot before leaving the think box. If you have confidence in yourself, you are less likely to change your mind the middle of it. The wrong time to doubt yourself is in the execution box, this will cause you to lose your momentum and second guess yourself. We also need to consider how we set ourselves up for the next shot, which is part of good course management. The execution box is the area where you do just that, execute your shot without thinking about it. Most people tend to get in the address position and start thinking about what to do next, as though they are waiting for Christmas. Then they tend to second guess themselves, and de-commit from their shot, which usually produces poor results. It is important to remember, NEVER THINK OVER THE BALL, if you find this happening, back away and start the process over.

When I was very young, I was afraid to dive head first from a diving board in fear of doing something known as a belly flop. If you've ever experienced it, you can certainly relate. It hurts! The problem was that I would see little girls half my size and age, diving head first like it was nothing. Being a guy and not wanting to look wimpy, I would muster up the courage to go through with it, no matter how much it hurt. I would make up my mind, and stand at the end of the diving board with full intentions of making the dive. However, once I would begin the process, fear would creep into my mind, and then I would try to back out of the dive. Since I was already in motion, it was too late to abort the dive. In an attempt to recover and get my feet to go first, I would end up flat onto the water, resulting in the belly flop. The pain incurred by it would reinforce my fear. The point here is that if we change our minds in the middle of an action, we end up de-committing from the action, resulting in something other than what we initially intended.

This happens the same way in the golf shot. Shot determination should never be done standing over the ball. While standing directly behind the ball, pick an item or a distinguished spot in front of the ball, about (twelve to sixteen) inches.

This is the same strategy that a bowler uses. Advanced bowlers don't aim at pins, they aim at marks. With that thought, the golfer can use a broken tee, a weed, a divot, or anything else. It's just a point of reference in our peripheral view that we can see while looking at our ball in the address position. It's important that the point of reference not be too close to the front of the ball. Using less distance sets you up for more error in alignment. At close range one degree of error may seem insignificant; however at a greater distance it can be huge.

Another thing to consider when teeing up is where you tee your ball. When looking down the fairway, find the most desirable area for the ball to land. The thought is to tee it up on the opposite side.

This gives you more of a margin for error, a wider landing area, minimizes the hazards and helps in taking the undesirable area out of play.

Another thing that you have to consider is how you typically hit the ball. Based on whether you fade or draw the ball, this will determine the landing area as well as the side of the teeing area that you'll use in your shot.

After taking all of this information into consideration, I visualize the shot in my mind; then set myself into position and begin the process. This even comes down to how and where I position myself behind the ball. I have my weight on my right foot with my forward hand starting the grip at my side. The distance from the ball is always the same too. Remember, it's all about routine! I have memorized an exact distance of seven feet from my toes to the ball. While standing relaxed behind the ball, I can even imagine exactly where my feet will be at address.

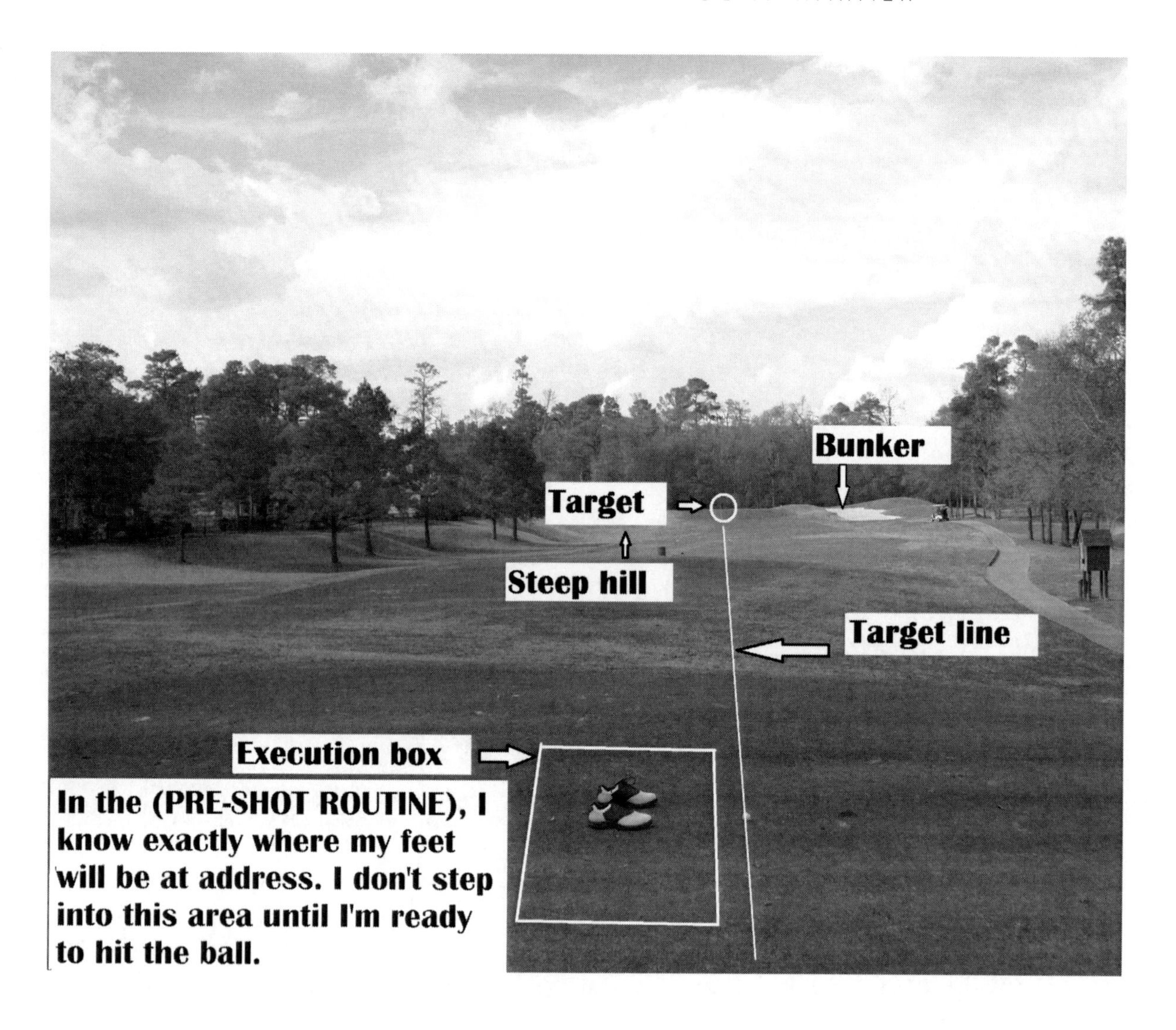

It's as though my shoes are actually in position, and I'm going to just step into them. Once I go through my thought process and I've committed to my shot, I take a series of five steps to the address position, which I count off in my mind. I start off with my left foot as step number one, and at the same time, I lift the club to place my other hand on the grip.

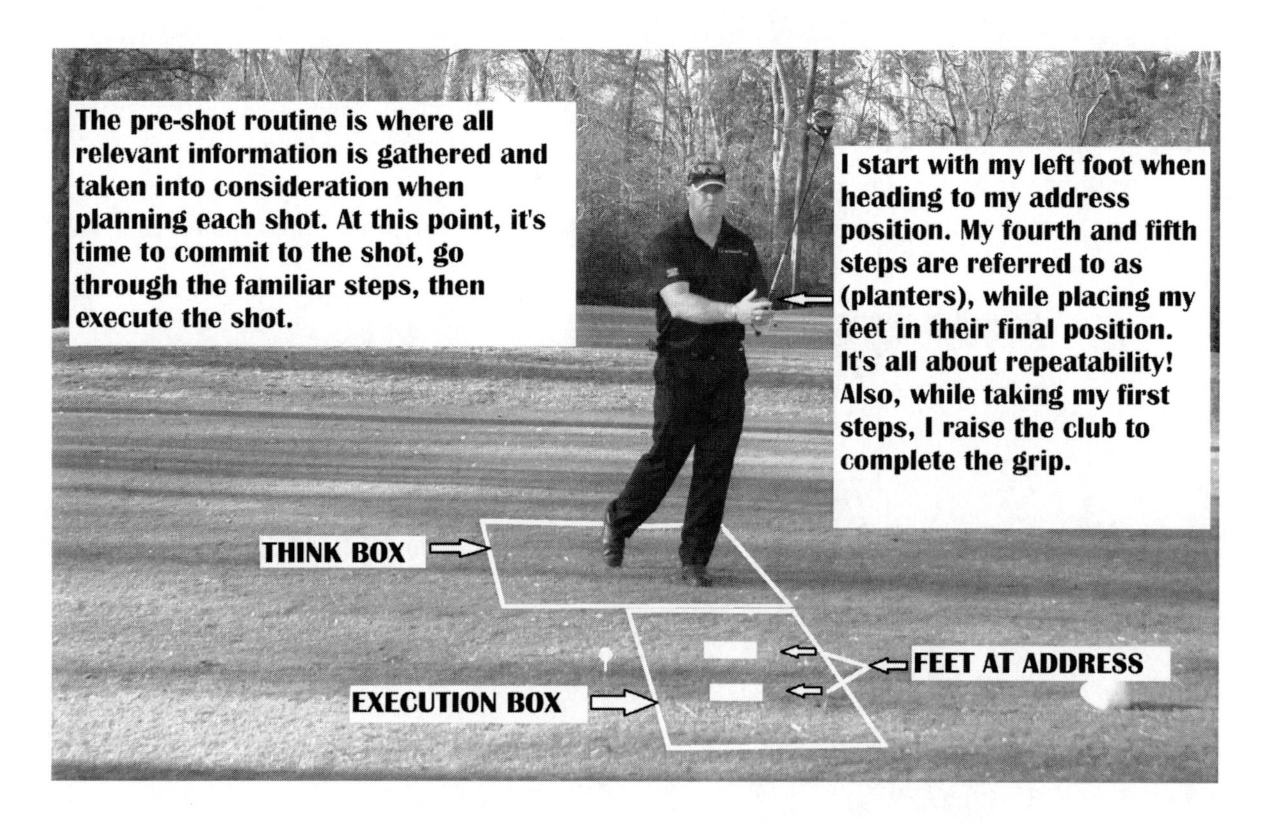

As a helpful tip, you'll find that with the club in a vertical position in front of your face, it's much easier to place the second hand correctly on the club. From there, I count out my steps with my fourth and fifth step referred to as planters. Once I'm in position, I do what's known as a waggle.

I do that twice, and then I let it go. The purpose of a waggle is simply to remove tension and stress from the hands and arms, as well as to reassure which fingers in the grip are actually being used. Remember, it's all about the three and two fingers in the grip. The three fingers holding with the forward hand and two fingers with the rear hand. When I waggle, I actually open up a large C in my rear hand with the index finger and thumb to reassure the proper fingers are being used during the shot to avoid choking/strangling the club.

SWING MECHANICS

Now that we've gone through the thought process and figured what type of shot we want to make, and where we want to land, it's time to actually look at the swing itself. I am going to take you through the swing by breaking it down to the basic elements, while explaining each component and how they contribute to the swing. There are three movements in the swing: vertical, lateral, and rotational. There are also seven parts of the swing: the address, backswing or takeaway, top of the swing, downswing, impact, the follow through, and the finish. Since we've gone through everything to the address position, we'll start with the moving parts of the swing. So here we go.

THE TAKEAWAY

The first part of the swing is commonly known as the takeaway, or frequently referred to as the backswing, which should be performed in a one piece takeaway. A one piece takeaway is simply the beginning of the swing, which is performed with the turn of the shoulders, and core of the body, with the arms remaining constant on the way back.

This is important because it sets the club on plane while keeping the clubface square relative to the swing path.

As simple as this may seem, many individuals struggle with it. Your head needs to remain constant while your shoulders, arms, and hands wind up.

The back leg should be the stable foundation to support your weight as you move back. The forward arm should remain extended, but not particularly locked; and the rear elbow should be down relative to the spine angle.

The role of the rear arm at this time is to support the club. If the back elbow is not kept low and in toward the torso or ribs, you will end up with something known as a *flying elbow*.

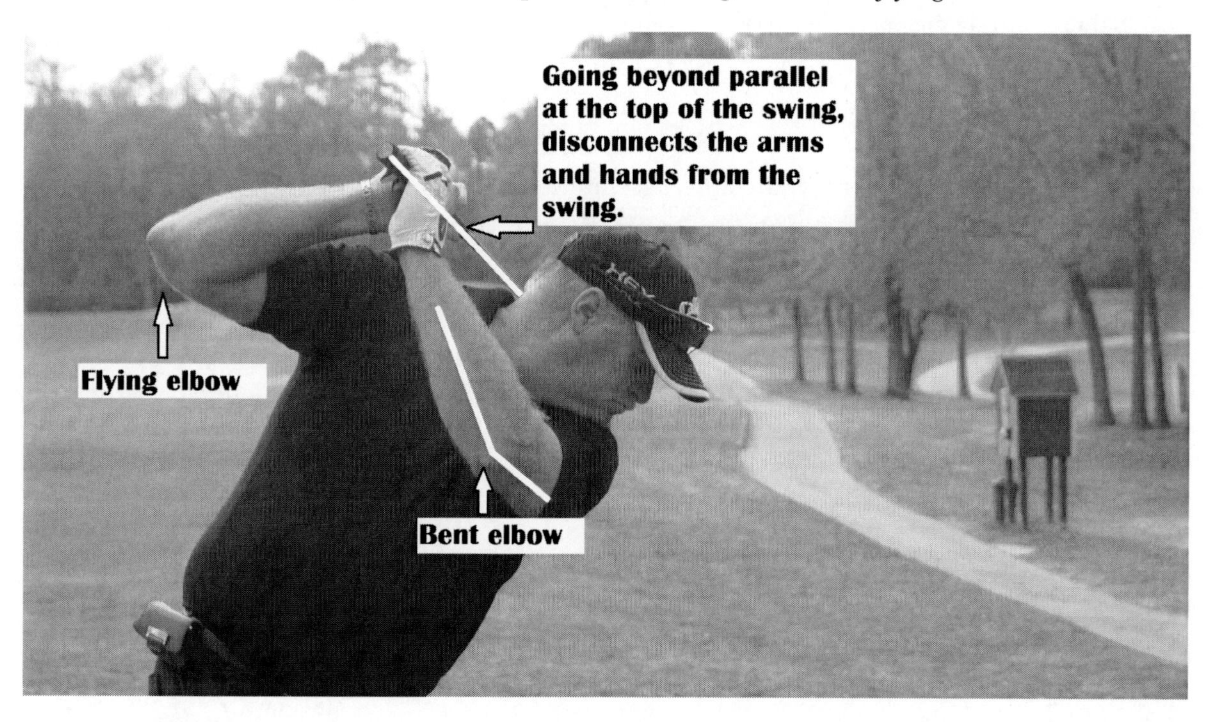

An easy way to remember this is imagine taking the clubhead back and putting it into a baseball catcher's mitt.

If the one piece takeaway is performed correctly, a down the line observer would see the toe of the club leaning slightly forward with the grip pointing directly at the target in the parallel position. Parallel simply means the point in the swing where the club is parallel to the ground. The club should remain in front of the body to a certain point. This indicates proper turning of the body. That thought will assist in bringing the clubhead low and slow, while promoting a wide arc when bringing the club back. Remember, to keep your hands as far from you as possible. Think of the perimeter of a tire. The larger the circumference in the rotation of any object, around another, the more distance it will travel, which equates to more speed. That works the same way in your swing.

SECOND HALF OF BACKSWING

Continuing up in the swing, the club should begin to cock with the forward/dominant wrist,

which is similar to cocking a hammer ready to strike a nail. The forward wrist should remain flat or slightly bowed. Something very important to remember, if you were hammering a nail into a board, you would not hold the hammer with a bent or cupped wrist. You would never get the nail into the board. Your dominant wrist acts as a lever, and needs to be straight in order to efficiently strike the nail.

This same principle applies to the golf swing, because you are actually making the same movement in the swing. The reason I am mentioning this is people are unaware they cup their forward wrist, which hinders their swing.

In general, if the forward wrist is cupped at the top of the swing, the face of the club will be closed, relative to the swing path.

If a correction is not made prior to impact, it will typically lead to a hooked or pulled shot. Other contributing factors that result in a hook shot are the hands out running the hips, over rotation of the hands, and lack of body rotation through impact and beyond. On the other hand, excessively bowing the forward wrist renders the clubface open relative to the swing path, which also requires correction prior to impact to avoid a slice. These two extremes are variables which add unnecessary movements to the swing. A slice can also be caused by the hips out running the hands, or failure to properly release the club at impact.

Other key factors to remember are: weight transfer, proper rotation of the shoulders and hips, and maintaining a steady head. What you do not want is to turn and lean back when you are loading the swing. The loading actually ends up in the rear hip, which means you have transferred your weight away from the target, but have not swayed back. This allows you to maintain a loaded position ready to thrust forward.

When you reach the top of your swing, if done correctly, the upper portion of your back should be facing the target with the forward arm extended, and the club should be over your rear shoulder. It is important to know when and where to stop.

This is a full turn in the backswing. Notice how my back is facing the target, the forward arm is extended for width, my weight is loaded onto the rear leg, and my head is behind the ball. The club is pointing at the target at the top of the swing.

Too many people believe that the farther they go back in the swing, the farther the ball with travel. This however is a myth. What people fail to realize is, once they reach a certain point in their backswing—which is really based on their flexibility—that should be it. Going beyond that will disconnect them from the swing, lead to inconsistent shots, as well as set them up for potential injuries.

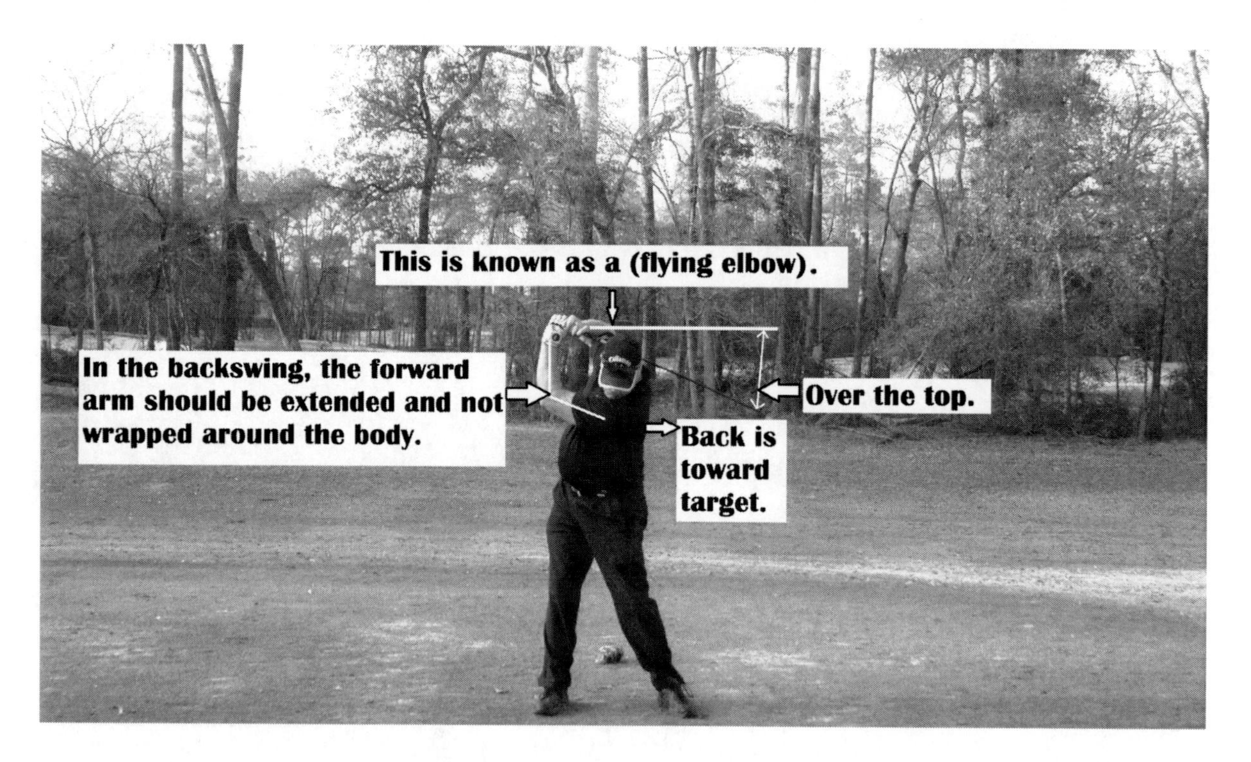

The degree of the turn should be limited to how far they can comfortably rotate, and still maintain proper control of the club. Going too far back, usually leads to breaking the established angle and the loss of leverage.

Truthfully, all you really need is to achieve an angle just above the top of the shoulder, which allows you to be as aggressive as needed without disconnecting. During this process, you should achieve a certain angle between the forward arm and the club, which is known as a static angle, or more commonly referred to as, *the angle*. This is similar to cocking a hammer.

DOWNSWING TO ALMOST IMPACT

The downswing is where the hips, shoulders, arms, and hands change direction and start to unwind. This is also where the forward transfer of weight actually begins. Remember, the swing is executed from the ground up. There are some players who lift their forward heel slightly off the ground at the top of their swing, due to limited flexibility or a bad back. For those players who do, that's no problem, but the first thing you should do in the downswing is plant the forward heel. From there, the sequence of the swing is to kick the forward knee toward the target, rotate the hips, torso, shoulders, arms, hands, and then the club. So as you can see, the swing is executed from the ground up.

There should be an angle between the club and the forward arm. Although, this angle is established during the backswing, it is maintained during the downswing until the hands reach the area of the rear pocket. This is known as *lag*.

Something else I want to point out is that the rear shoulder will get closer to the hip on the way down. This is known as *body compression*, and is where the power in the swing becomes intensified and released through impact.

Thinking back to a time, when you have seen a figure skater twirling in one spot, they would begin to spin at a certain speed with their arms extended. However, when retracting their arms, bringing them closer to the body, being the center axis, the rate of spin would increase proportionally. This would continue until they extended their arms out and away from their torso, thus widened the circumference of the body, decelerating the rate of spin, and eventually coming to a stop. This simple principal of physics works the same way in a golf swing. This principal works because energy is condensed through body compression in the swing, and if applied correctly should be released just prior to impact. The energy never leaves the object, it's only redirected.

At the point in time when your hands reach the rear pocket area, the release begins, and hand rotation takes place. When the clubhead reaches the point of impact, it should be square to the target. The forward arm should be fully extended, as one with the club shaft, and your forward wrist straight. The back wrist should be cupped and the palm square to the target. Although the release is commonly referred to as a single component or movement, there are actually two releases that take place in the swing. One, being the elimination of the angle established between the forward arm and the club shaft, and the second, being the rotation of the clubhead through impact. Both must happen simultaneously in order to square the clubhead at impact.

Something I want to bring to your attention is the similarity between the address and impact positions. What this simply means is the address position is merely establishing where you want to be at impact.

This is the perfect time to bring up another point. I can't tell you how many players take their address position with the clubhead several inches behind the ball, then hit a fat shot and can't figure out why. Remember, address is establishing a point of return. So you want to place the clubhead right behind the ball when addressing it.

THE FOLLOW THROUGH

At this point in time, your weight should be transferred to the forward side, and the rear arm extended with the forward elbow starting to fold.

After impact, the rear arm should be extended and the hands fully rotated. The hips should also be rotated, with the head still over the impact zone. The weight should be completely transferred to the forward foot.

This will result in the forearms coming together, and the hands completing their rotation. Now I get a lot of baseball players who struggle with this part of the swing. The forward elbow tends to get away from the body and pull straight back.

This is caused by isolating the upper part of the body in the swing, resulting in what's referred to as a *chicken wing*. This is a breakdown in the swing, causing the hitter to cut across the ball resulting in a severe pull or duck hook. It also causes severe slices and toe shots, depending on the face angle.

In all of this, proper weight transfer is a must. When comparing this to other sports, think of throwing a baseball or a football. When you're throwing the ball to someone, you wouldn't keep your weight on the back foot, or even worse, start on the forward foot and move back. In golf this is referred to as a *reverse pivot*. You'd be surprised with the vast number of people that struggle with this. The swing itself is simply energy created by the body, which is directed and transferred through the arms, hands, shaft, clubhead, and ultimately into the ball.

The objective is to time the release where it happens in what we call the impact zone, or the *moment of truth*. As you continue your rotation and the proper turning of your hips, you should end up with your belt buckle toward the intended target.

This is an indication you have allowed your body to finish the swing, resulting in the transition of your weight to the forward foot, and the back foot should end up on the toe.

If this is done correctly, you will be able to lift your rear foot without losing your balance.

Some players, including myself, slightly drag the instep of the rear foot to the finished position. This is an indication that all of the weight has been transferred to the forward side. It is important to practice good tempo and accelerate through the swing, which will result in crisp clean shots. This is how you maintain control needed to achieve favorable results. Something I want to elaborate on is the finish position. The goal is to simply find a relaxed, balanced, comfortable, and repeatable position; practice the pose, then practice going to it. It needs to be natural, and you have to trust it. Once this is accomplished, it becomes easy.

I have my students imagine there is a camera lens on their belt buckle, and the only way an observer can see their beautiful shot is through the lens. It's important that their belt buckle be pointed directly at the target, and extended forward at least as far as the nose. At the finish of the swing, you don't want to have the upper body leaning beyond the front foot toward the target. If the upper body exceeds the front foot, you will feel as though you are losing your balance. Leaning too far forward is usually caused by lazy hips and is an indication of an incomplete turn. It also helps if at address, you point the front foot outward, generally five to ten degrees or so, which will alleviate stress on the forward knee.

A helpful drill that was shown to me many years ago is to take a soccer ball, and place it in the palm of your hands with your arms extended. Take the address position as if you were taking a normal shot. While simulating the backswing the forward hand should rotate over the rear hand, and your weight should shift in the same direction.

From there, shift your weight forward while turning the body and rotate your hands in the opposite direction, delivering the ball to the target. What this drill does is promote the feeling of the hands, body, and weight shift being synchronized in the swing.

Another good drill is to visualize someone on your rear side holding a tray of water, while someone on your forward side desires it. This would simply be performed by extending the arms, turning the body toward the rear side, then taking the tray and merely turning in the opposite direction. While maintaining an upright and balanced position, hand the tray to the other person. This keeps the weight inside the feet and avoids the feeling of tipping over in either direction. Remember, the turning is done with the body and not the arms. The swing is exactly the same. It's relaxed and achieved with the turning of the body.

RHYTHM

If there is anything that can absolutely ruin a great swing, it's poor rhythm. I see far too many players take the club back abruptly, then at the top of their swing, violently change the direction of the club by jerking it back down to the ball. This is known as pulling the trigger.

Or, they go back slowly, and swing at full speed trying to instantly achieve one hundred percent of their clubhead speed. This is similar to that of an archer. When shooting a bow and arrow, the archer will pull the arrow back slowly, then suddenly release it, thus shooting the arrow at full speed. It's important to remember though, speed is attained through acceleration. Maximum clubhead speed should be just beyond impact.

Good tempo is vital if you have any hope of making a smooth and effective swing. It needs to be a pendulous motion, and not hurried. This gives all segments of the swing a chance to do their part. It also allows you to fully wind and release in the swing.

Tension is usually the culprit of jerky motions; however, if you want to be consistent in cleanly striking the ball, you must maintain good tempo. Proper weight shift and body turn depends on it. A good way to check for good tempo in your swing is to take a piece of rope, swing it like a club, while attempting to keep it straight.

If you jerk in one direction or the other, it will fold or buckle. Think of the club in the same way. It's all about the weight at the end of the stick.

If at any time you lose that sensation, you can simply take a club, flip it around, hold the headed end (of the shaft) in your hands, and swing it a few times, then simply flip the club back around to the correct position, and swing it a few more times. This will help you regain the proper sensation while making you aware of the weight at the end of the club.

COURSE MANAGEMENT

Good course management actually starts during the pre-shot routine. It's the continuous thought process that takes place during the entire round, staying one or two steps ahead as one would do in a chess game, while navigating around the course. As you make your way down the fairway, the thought process continues while making any necessary adjustments.

Course management is simply gathering relevant information, considering your options, and building a strategy that best fits the situation. It is also thinking ahead, so each shot will leave you in a favorable position for the next.

This is how good billiard players think. Beyond hitting the ball into the pocket, the player needs to hit the shot in a way so the cue ball will be in a good position for the next shot. That's how they run the table. This is where knowing how to work the golf ball really comes into play, and helps you successfully navigate the course by helping you maneuver through and around obstacles.

This continues until the ball is holed out. Taking the time to use good course management and thinking through each shot will always produce a better score.

Another essential element of good course management is self-management. It's important to drink plenty of fluids to remain hydrated, and keep something healthy to snack on like fruit or crackers.

This helps by maintaining good blood sugars levels, and sufficient energy, which assists in the ability to think clearly. Additionally, it's important to properly stretch before and during your round to avoid possible injuries.

SIDE-, UP-, AND DOWNHILL SHOTS

Uneven terrain—we see that more often than we realize. We usually practice in a designated area where there is always a perfect or level lie, but when we get onto the actual course, we rarely see the same thing. Players wonder why shots work on the practice tee, but not on the course. Well, that's why. So let's talk about that.

Hitting these shots is not as difficult as people may think. There are, however, certain factors that should be taken into consideration. When looking down the fairway and making a club selection for the next shot, you usually chose the club that has a certain loft and or distance associated with it, again this is based on ideal conditions. This is where it can become tricky, because when the terrain is un-level, it changes the characteristic of the club. When calculating this shot, you will need to determine the severity of the slope to select a club that best fits the situation.

If you are hitting the ball when it is positioned above your feet, you will notice that the ball will tend to travel in a direction more behind you.

The more severe the slope is, the more offline it will go. In addition, the more loft the club has, the more the angle is exaggerated, and you will need to adjust your direction to compensate for this. An option to consider is to choke down on the club, so you can maintain an upright and balanced position during the swing. However, this may not always be a viable option in certain circumstances. Another point to consider is when shortening the club with the ball above the feet, it will affect the lie angle of the clubhead, relative to the slanted hitting surface. In other words, the toe will hit the ground before the heel. Now, with a shorter club, you'll have to use a less lofted club to make up for the lost distance.

Just the opposite, if you find yourself in a situation where the ball is below your feet,

it will tend to go in a direction more in front of you after being struck, and the heel will hit the ground first. This will also affect the length of the club as well. With this scenario however, it's better to bend a little more at the knees, bringing you closer to the ball, while maintaining a balanced position. If the slope is severe, an option to consider is to find a safe landing area, which will set you up for the next shot. This will save some strokes in the long run.

If you find your ball on a downhill slope, the best way to handle this shot is to contour to the slope, and maintain a balanced position with the majority of your weight on the forward leg. This will give you a solid foundation for your swing. Remember, your trajectory will be affected, so take a more lofted club to make up the difference. A more lofted club is also a shorter club, which takes distance away, so keep that in mind. This leaves one more slope, the uphill shot.

You want to contour to the slope, and maintain the majority of your weight on the back or lower leg, which acts as a solid foundation for the swing. You'll need to use a less lofted club and choke down on it; which shortens it and takes a few yards back. As with all irregular situations, spend time practicing different shots to determine what works best for you.

SCORING ZONE—FIFTY YARDS AND IN

This is where the money is usually made. Fifty yards and in is what's known as the scoring zone. There's nothing worse than hitting a great drive, and then chunking the ball or hitting it fat on your approach shot to waste a stroke or two; and perhaps, even end up in a worse position than before you hit.

Of course, a little thought and preparation can avoid this from happening.

There are really three basic types of shots. The pitch, the chip, and the flop shot. Keep in mind as a rule of thumb though, the loftier the shot, the riskier the shot. Why is that?

The loftier the shot means a higher ball flight with the least room for error—the loftier the club, the steeper the angle, the smaller the actual hitting area of the clubface. When deciding which club to use, these facts need to be considered. Depending on the flange of the club, you also risk the leading edge of the clubface bouncing off the ground and hitting into the equator of the ball. This is commonly referred to as sculling the ball. Additionally, this tends to promote flipping the club, which results in inconsistencies.

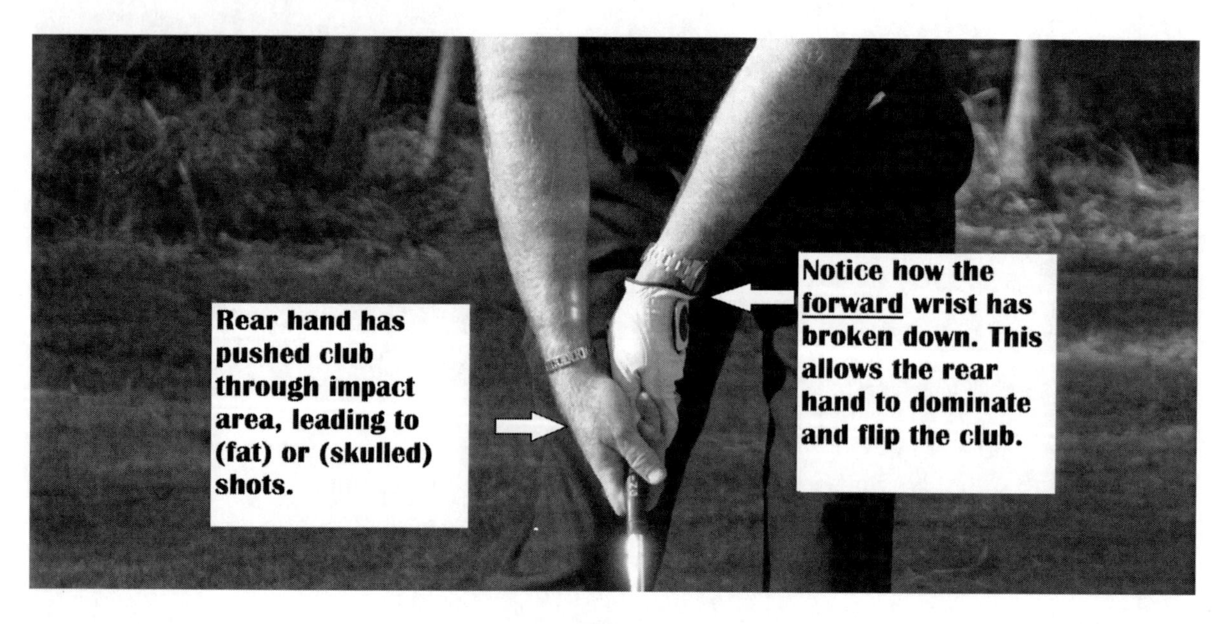

This all comes down to a percentage shot, depending on how far you are from the putting surface, and how much green there is to work with. This is the point in time the decision is made, whether you want to chip or pitch.

With very little landing area to work with, open the stance, choke down on the club, open the face, and stand with the club a little more verticle rather than with a forward lean. Slide the club face under the ball and avoid decelerating.

Whichever shot you take, it is extremely important that you maintain a constant speed; or if anything, slightly accelerate the club through the shot, and be certain to finish the stroke. The difference between pitching and chipping is, pitching travels farther in the air than it does on the ground; whereas, chipping, also known as “bump and run” shots, travel farther on the ground than in the air. The goal is to get the ball on the putting surface as soon as possible. With these shots, your hands should be positioned ahead of the ball at address.

This de-lofts the club and greatly increases the hitting area. This will also increase the odds of striking the ball clean.

Now, when it comes down to the longer pitches being, twenty, thirty, forty or even fifty yards, it's helpful to imagine time positions of a clock, which can be used as a reference to gage how high to elevate your hands in the swing. Each time position will produce a particular distance. *(See next page)* For instance, if using a sand wedge, and elevating the club to the eight o'clock position, it produces a twenty-yard shot, whereas eight-thirty may produce thirty yards, nine o'clock may produce forty yards, and so on.

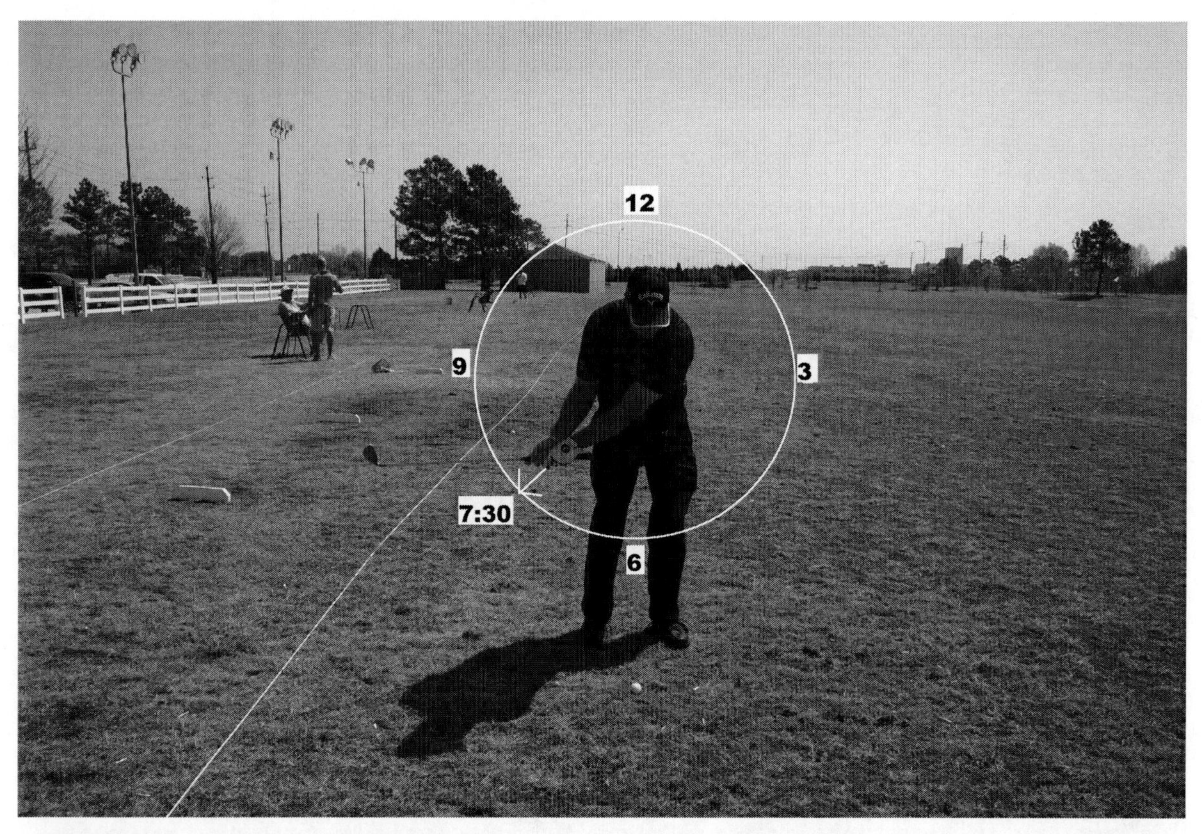
12
9
3
7:30
6

12
9
3
4:30
6

If you change to another iron an duplicate the shot, it will produce different results because of the characteristics of the club, such as loft and travel distances. So, it's important to spend time with different clubs to determine what they will do for you. Remember, you don't want to change your swing; just use different time positions of the clock to produce the desired distance. It is also important to remember that the follow through in the swing should mirror the backswing. If you take the club back to the nine o'clock position, the follow through should end at the three o'clock position, etc.

CHIPPING AND PITCHING

How many times have you taken a shot on a par three, or an approach shot from the fairway; finding yourself just off the green? It happens more often than you think. Even tour players find themselves facing this situation quite often. Now, people usually spend a lot of time practicing their normal shots; but the truth is, the short game is usually what eats them up. They find themselves next to the green on their second shot, on a par four hole, and end up with a seven or eight; because they couldn't get up and down or recover from the miss.

After a couple holes like this, they are ready to give up, feeling as though their round is ruined. With a little thought and some practice though, this can all be avoided. I'm going to share a few options that will help you get through this. To begin with, you want to remember that all shots should end up with your weight on the forward side, and if you are making a shorter shot, there should be little or no weight transfer in the swing. Due to this fact, the ideal way to make this shot is to begin and end with your weight on the forward side. This allows the lower body to remain very quiet, meaning minimal body movement. Your feet should be very close together, and your body should feel as though it is leaning toward the target. When chipping the ball, it is important to maintain the angle established between the wrist and club throughout the entire shot, (no flipping). After striking the ball, your hands should still be ahead of the clubhead at the finish. This is an indication you did not release the club. This shot is similar to putting, which is the easiest shot in the bag, where the hands remain firm, and do not flip through the shot. An easy drill to insure that your hands do not release through impact, is to take a rod or an extension of the shaft, and address the ball while leaning the club forward in the direction of the target. From there, take your shot while ensuring the extension does not hit you in the side.

This will force you to turn with the hips and keep your hands ahead through the shot.

When you find yourself off the putting surface and around the green, here are some options to help determine which club to use. When breaking the distance down into parts, "fly versus roll." Use this general formula to decide which club to use: two parts fly—one part roll, use a lob wedge; one part fly—one part roll, use the sand wedge; one part fly—two parts roll, use a pitching wedge; one part fly—three parts roll, and so on. This formula may vary with each player, and time should be spent practicing to see what works best for you.

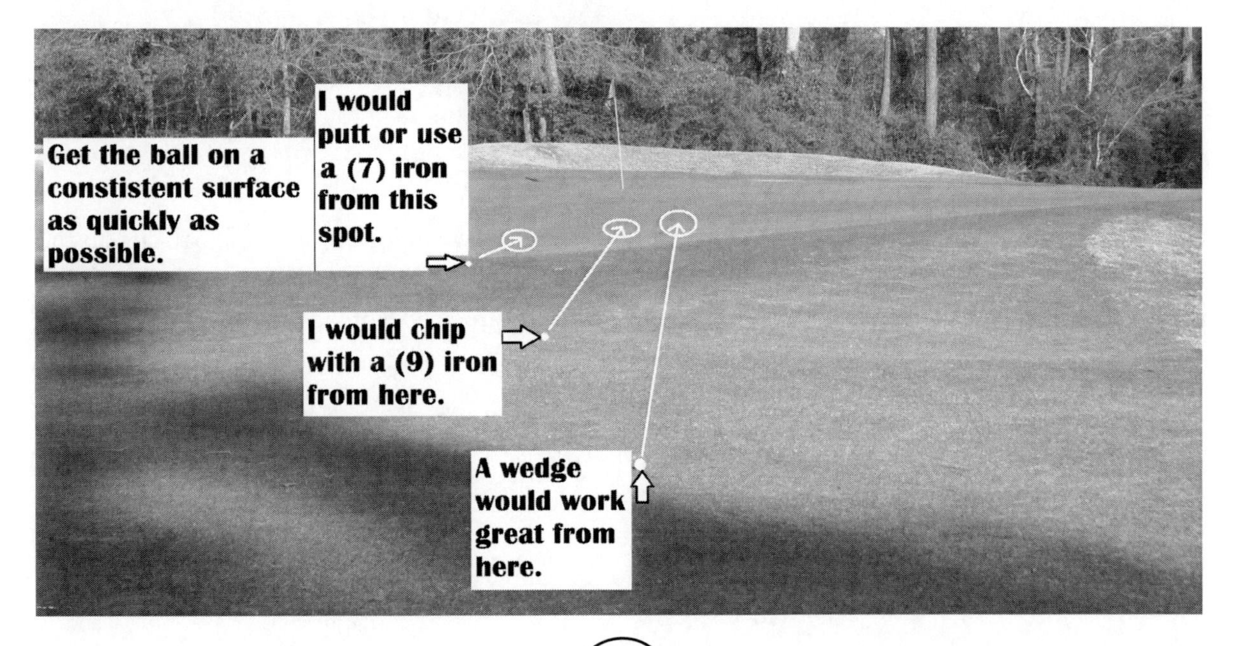

It is important to take notes with each shot to determine what each club will produce. Something that will assist you with shorter chip shots is to purposely position the hands slightly farther away from the body than normal, causing the clubhead to be slightly "toe deep" when striking the ball, this is known as *nipping*. The reason for this is to reduce the friction on the bottom edge of the clubhead when striking the ball.

The body alignment and ball placement will vary, depending on personal preference. The determining factors are: (1) the lie, (2) the terrain, (3) the line of sight, (4) the loft of the club,

and (5) your landing options. So let's break these down. You have to look at how the ball sits on the turf and how accessible it is. Is it in high grass, or on closely cut grass? This is what will determine how you strike the ball. If it is in short grass you can easily make clean contact, depending on the loft and distance needed, you can make a fairly normal shot.

When the ball is sitting in high grass, or in a divot and difficult to make clean contact with, you will need to use a steeper angle of approach, resulting in a more descending blow.

This will minimize the amount of grass that will be caught between the clubface and the ball. You will need to use a more lofted club as well, which will allow the clubface to knife through the grass and make cleaner contact. With both of these shots, be sure to choke down on the club, making it easier to control. Also, be conscious of the fact that a more lofted club will travel a shorter distance, so you will need to adjust accordingly.

Second, you will need to determine whether the ball is on a slope or on a level lie. This will affect the angle of approach into the ball. Keep in mind, the one thing that doesn't change is the direction of gravity. So if you are on a slope, you will have to remember to add the loft of the club to the degree of slope, and the feet should be fairly close to each other due to little, or no lower body movement in the swing. So set yourself to where the upper body conforms to the slope and make a relatively normal shot. Remember to keep your weight forward.

Third, if you find yourself in a position where you can't see the landing area or even the pin, the best thing to do is to take the time, walk up to the green and determine a good landing area, one that will leave you in a favorable position, after the ball comes to rest.

With blind or obscured shots, walk onto the green and pick a landing spot prior to hitting the ball. This will avoid any surprises.

The loft of the club will make a huge different in the outcome. The idea is to stand in a position on the green just off the flight-line, between the ball and the pin, to determine the best landing area.

The two most important factors to consider are, the distance the ball will roll, and the direction it will go after landing. This will increase your chances of a favorable result.

BUNKER/SAND-TRAP

The bunker is also commonly referred to as a sand-trap. This is a hazard that most amateurs fear and try to avoid because they view it as punishment for a bad shot. They would rather land short, or risk hitting over the green, than to land in the sand. However, what they fail to realize is the bunker shot is relatively easy. Some tour players will even aim for the bunker as a safe alternative. Advanced players will even try to hole, or at least land close to the pin.

The basic concept for most sand shots is the same. However, the characteristics will change based on the distance and loft needed. For instance, on a greenside bunker, where more loft and less distance is needed, you would take more sand, and a steeper approach into the ball. Whereas, with a fairway bunker you would avoid hitting the sand and attempt to pick the ball clean. I'm going to share how to execute the basic shot out of the bunker, explain why it works, and then look at the two most common scenarios you might find yourself in. The two extremes are a ball sitting on the sand, and a ball buried in the sand. There are basic approaches for each shot. Two important factors to also keep in mind when determining your shot are whether you are in a greenside or fairway bunker, and how high the lip is that you have to clear.

When hitting from a greenside bunker, you will need to determine how open the face is as well as the path of the clubhead. The basic shot is generally the same, and I'll show you what I mean. Now, it's a good idea to take practice swings before entering the bunker, because it is a violation of the rules to ground the club, or touch the surface while in a hazard, prior to taking the actual stroke. This is considered testing the surface.

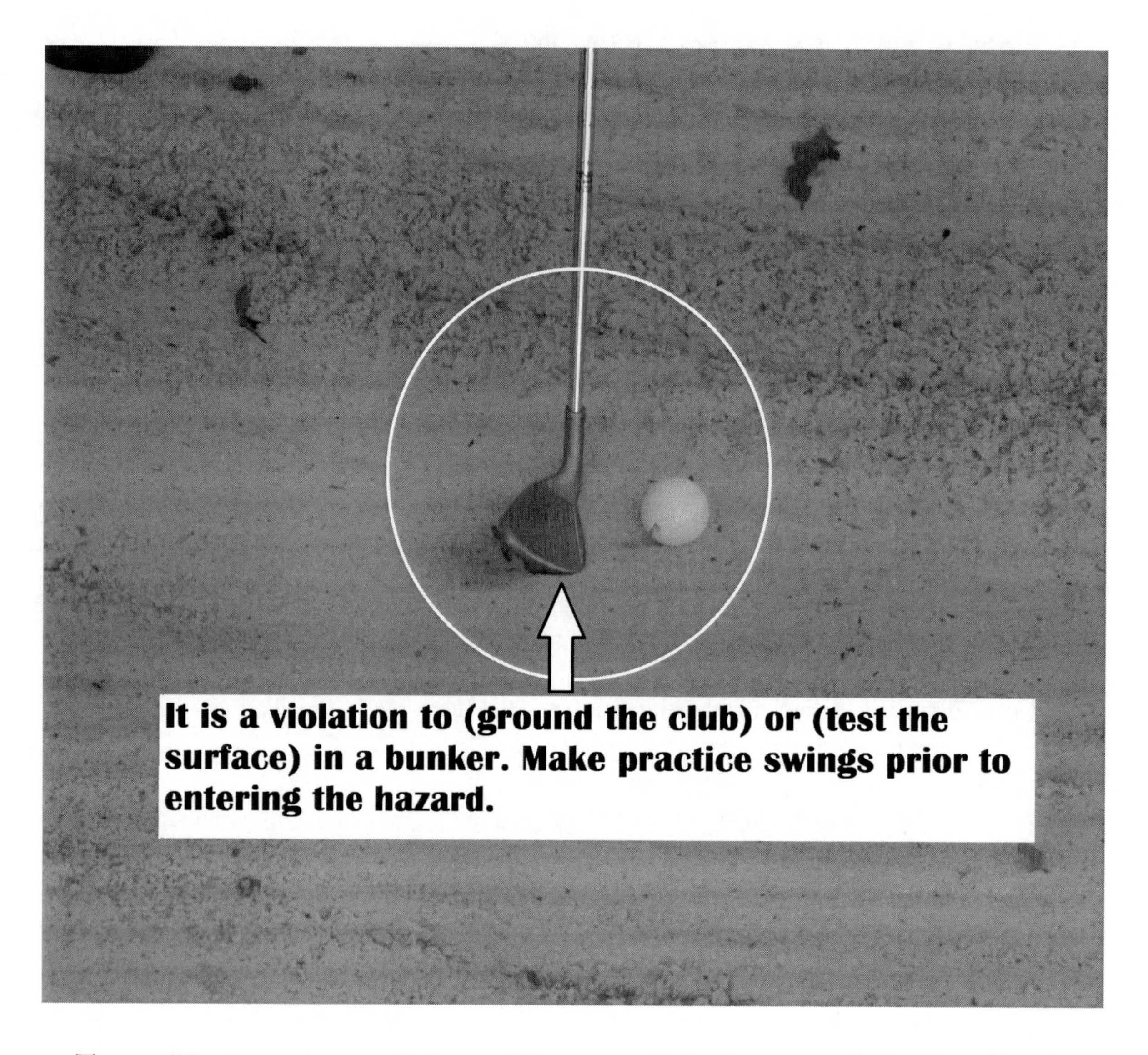

There will be times when you find yourself in a greenside bunker, in which the desired ball flight is high and with little travel distance. This is usually in a situation where the ball needs to clear a high lip and then roll a very short distance after landing. This is actually an easy shot if you follow these simple steps. Depending on the distance needed to accommodate the shot, you will need to address the ball in an opened stance with your body alignment at an angle of up to 30 degrees relative to the target line.

Then, simply open the face of the club, and regardless of the angle, it is important that you remember to swing along your body-line and not toward the target. The more opened the stance, the less distance the ball will travel. Your weight should be just forward of center, and the ball forward in the stance with your knees in a forward direction. It is important to keep your weight centered because you will be entering the ground a couple inches behind the ball. You must take a full swing, accelerate through the shot and follow through to a finished position.

If you find that you need more distance in the shot, simply reduce the angle of the stance, relative to the target line. Whichever shot you make, you must insure that the leading edge of the clubface is facing the intended target. In addition, you will need to put the club in the position you want, then take your grip. If you attempt to open the clubface with your hands at address, then take your shot this will result in the club and hands returning back to the normal position at impact, which is a closed position.

I can't tell you how many players I see hitting at the ball with all they have, only to jab the clubface into the sand. This is known as stabbing and is usually an indication of quitting in the shot.

Doing this will prevent you from getting the ball out of the bunker. When you watch experienced players hit these shots, you will notice they dig their feet into the sand while taking their stance. This is done for two reasons. First, is to stabilize the feet and body, and the other is to give them an indication of how soft or deep the sand is. It's the only legal way of testing the sand. When hitting a shot where the ball is sitting on top of the sand, you will want to keep your weight centered and play the ball slightly forward in the stance. You should enter the ground between two and three inches behind the ball with a more shallow approach, and the clubhead should leave the sand two or three inches beyond the ball.

The displaced sand should resemble the size of a dollar bill.

An easy way to picture this is to think of trying to remove the sand out from under the ball without actually moving it. Due to the curvature on the bottom of the club, known as the bounce,

the club will not allow you to go under the ball. The bottom of the club is like the front edge of a water ski in that it promotes an upward motion as it travels forward. The sand shot is like taking a hand full of sand, putting a ball in the middle of it, and throwing the sand onto the green.

Second, if the ball is buried deep in the sand we call it a, "*fried egg.*" The swing principles are the same; except, you'll need to play the ball a little farther back in the stance with your weight favoring your forward side, which will promote a steeper approach into the sand behind the ball.

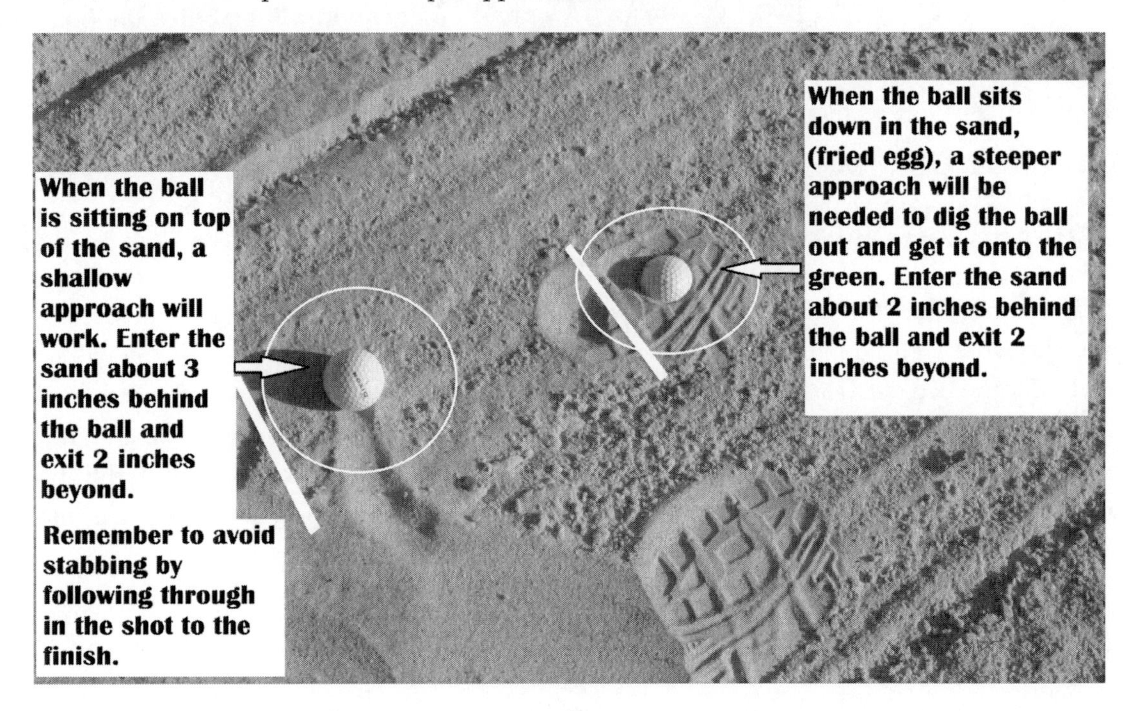

This will assist in digging the ball out and getting it up onto the green. Nevertheless, the main thing to remember is to confidently drive the club through the sand and finish the swing. Keep your knees pointing forward, and don't let the clubhead stick into the sand. Remember, always accelerate through the shot.

Now, if you find yourself in a fairway bunker, you're most likely going to have significant yardage left as well. This will be a little more like a normal shot than the greenside bunker in that you will not be trying to dig the ball out. This is usually a shot where you will try to cleanly pick the ball from the surface, avoiding resistance to the clubhead by the sand. That's provided you don't have a high lip to clear. You will want to take a few practice swings prior to entering the hazard to establish the apex, or bottom of your swing. This will dictate the best ball position for the shot. A level approach into the ball will work best.

Something else that you have to take into account is when you bury your feet in the sand; you will actually become a slight bit shorter relative to the ball position. The best way to compensate for this is to choke down a little on the club to make up the difference. Then just take a normal swing. If you do find that you have a high lip to clear, consider using a loftier club, taking a safer shot, and moving on. Otherwise, you could find yourself in a worse situation than when you started. It's all a part of good course management and recovery.

PUTTING

This is what it all leads to. You've done your work and gotten onto the putting surface. However, planning your putt actually starts before you even enter the green. As you approach the putting surface, you should already have an idea of what you want to do. You need to gather information as you approach the green, such as, the slopes, distance to the pin, the speed of the green, and the surrounding area that will have an influence on the outcome.

Something that you really want to consider is if there is any water in the area. Remember, water always runs downhill; and this will usually give you an indication of any downward influence on the ball. Once you are on the green, you can tell a lot just by walking on the surface, such as how soft the ground is. You should always make a complete circle around the putting surface due to the fact that you won't always see the break from any one spot.

You'll probably recall hitting a putt that didn't break the way you thought it would; and when you went to the other side, the true break was obvious.

Another thing that you'll notice is the turf will appear to be darker in one direction than another. That's because the blades of grass are leaning a certain way, usually downhill or following the sun, depending on the type of grass used. So, if it has sheen in the direction of the shot, this usually indicates that the putt will roll easier, with less resistance in that direction. If the grass appears dull, indicating you are putting against the grain, you will experience more resistance, and the ball will roll less. This same thought process can be used to determine the break of the ball from one side to the other.

Another way of determining slope is to walk up to the cup, and look at the edges.

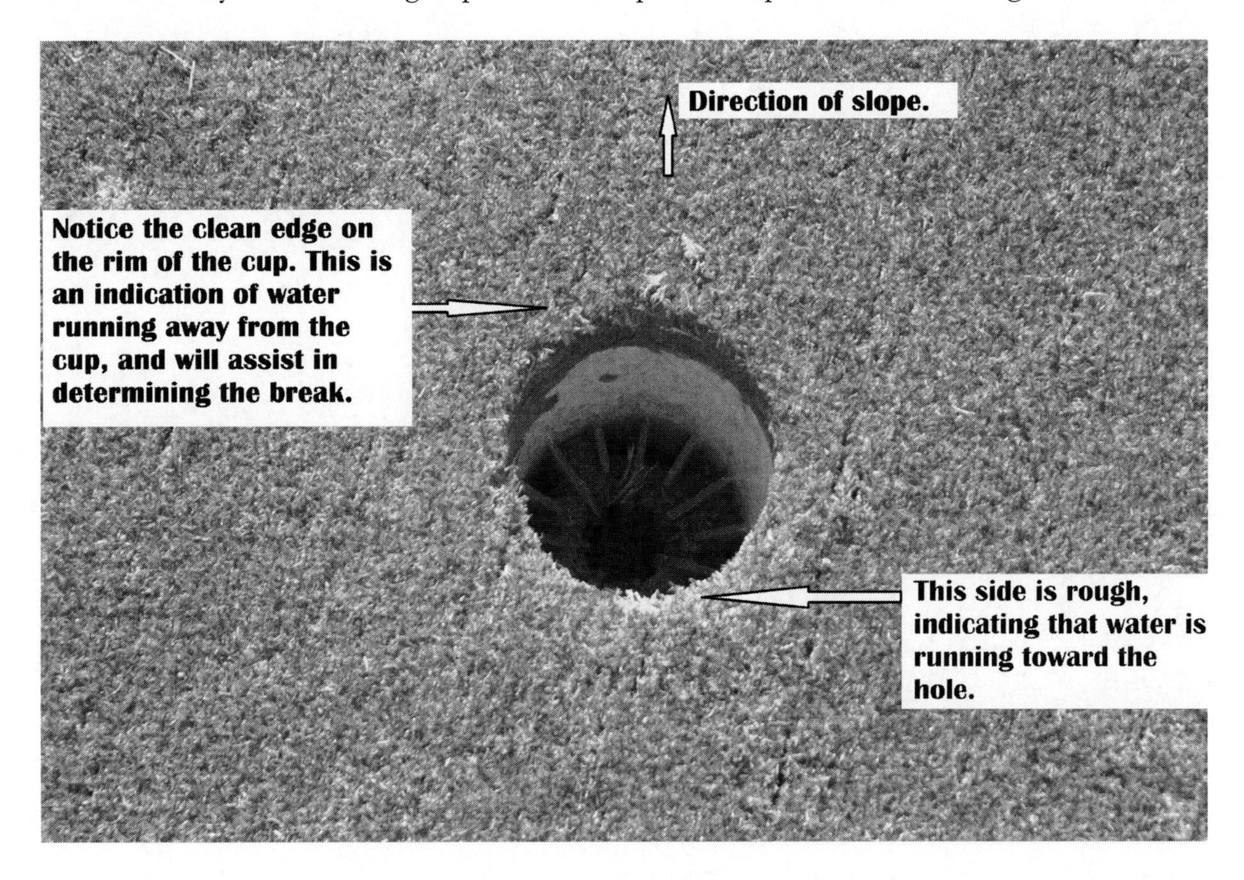

Chances are one edge will be fuzzy, and the other side will be clean cut. This is a great indication of slope and water flow, as well.

Once you have gathered your information prior to addressing the ball, take a few practice strokes to determine how hard you'll need to hit it for that particular distance.

This, like anything else, is where a lot of practice pays off. One thing that I've noticed is that some players tend to change putters when they struggle.

The truth is, if they would spend time learning and practicing the correct stroke, they would experience greater consistently and trust with their putts, and be less likely to feel the need to change equipment.

Putting is a very balanced and pendulous motion with virtually no body movement involved. The stroke should be performed with the shoulders and both arms working together as one. This promotes consistency for a truer path. Here are some good drills for developing a true swing-path. Tie a string to the top of two long tees, then fully extend and insert them into the ground. This will help establish a straight line to be used as a guide. Place your putter head under the string and then take some practice stokes.

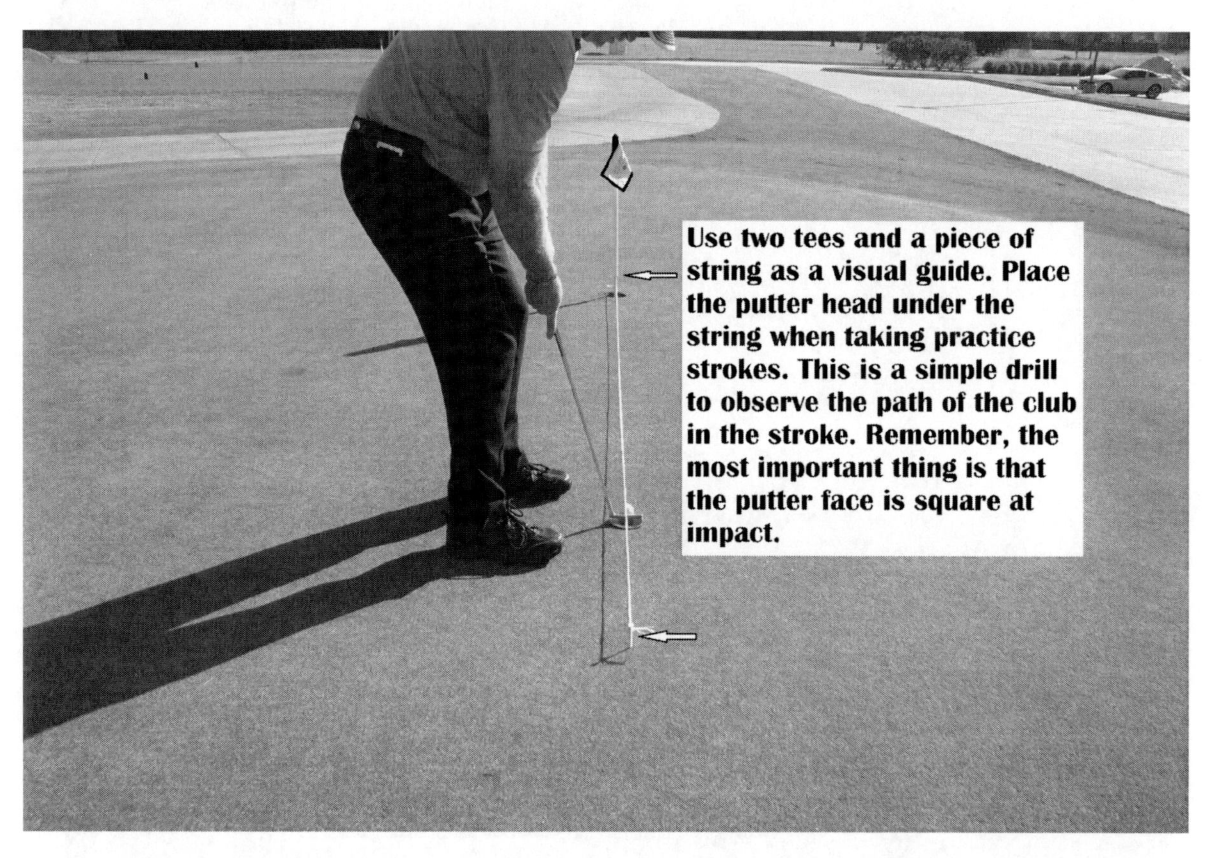

Another easy way to create a straight line of reference is to use a carpenters' chalk line, which can be found at most hardware stores, and since it uses a powdered chalk, it leaves no permanent marks or lines on the ground. With the putting stroke, some individuals prefer a straight clubhead path while others prefer a slight arc, this is based on an individual style or preference and both are acceptable. What really matters though is that the face is square at impact. Also, remember putting is done with the shoulders and not the body. A great way to acquire this feel is to place a club across your chest and under each arm when taking practice strokes. This helps isolate the shoulders from the body, and prevents swaying or turning. When done correctly, the ends of the club should rock straight up and down.

This drill helps reassure that the stroke is being made with the shoulders and not the hands.
It is very important that you maintain a consistent angle with the wrists throughout the stroke. Whether you prefer slightly cupped or completely flat with the forward wrist, you want to avoid flipping during the stroke. Hold the putter lightly in the hands and strike the ball with a smooth and pendulous motion.
Stroke is performed with the shoulders.
Maintain original wrist position.

It is vital that you don't flip the wrists at any time. The entire shot is made from the shoulders.

Something that is commonly taught and found in many instruction books and magazines is; that when you take your address position, your eyes should be directly over the ball. This is not always true. There are people, who are true dextral, while others are cross dextral. That simply means if the dominant eye is the rear eye, you are cross dextral. If the forward eye is dominant, you are true dextral. So why is this important?

Well, with a cross dextral player, the bridge of the nose partially obstructs the view of the line. To find your dominant eye, simply have both eyes open, then pick any object in the distance, place a finger where it blocks the object. Close one eye and if the finger appears to move, the other eye is dominant.

So, if you are cross dextral, you should consider playing the ball with your eyes over an area about halfway between the ball and your toes.

If you are true dextral, meaning the dominant eye is the forward eye, your best position would be eyes over the ball.

Now like everything else, some people will disagree with this method, so I suggest that you try both, and see what works best for you.

The last thing you need to practice is different distances, hitting balls from five, ten, fifteen, and twenty feet. This will give you confidence in how hard to hit your shots. It is very important that you finish the stroke, and that you maintain a constant speed throughout the process. It's imperative that you not decelerate during the stroke. Make your stroke smooth and pendulous, ensuring that your hands don't push, jerk, or jab at the ball. This is referred to as the "yipps," which is a result of tension and nerves. A great visual aid when practicing long or lag putts is a Hula-Hoop, which can be placed around the cup.

When hitting long putts without it, the hole appears to be the size of a pinhead, however when a Hula-Hoop is placed around the hole, it appears more like the Grand Canyon. It's all about your perception, confidence and level of comfort. If you are comfortable you will commit to the shot.

Another drill that helps you develop the feel and distance needed in putting, is to take smooth strokes holding the club with just the rear hand. This is the hand you trust the most based on the fact that you do pretty much everything else with it, so it only makes sense to use that same hand when obtaining feel and sensitivity. However, it's important to remember that the normal putting stroke is done with the shoulders and not the hands. The body must remain very quiet throughout the stroke. Be certain that you slightly hover above the ground to avoid accidently hitting the surface with the putter head prior to striking the ball.

HYBRIDS

Hybrids are the newest generation of clubs. When I started playing golf in 1970, a standard set of clubs would range from a 2 iron up to a 9 iron. The set would also include a pitching, and sand wedge. Then you would have # 1, (driver) # 2, and # 3 (fairway) Persimmon woods, and a putter. That was your set of 14 clubs. Things have certainly changed over the years and the latest trend in golf equipment is Hybrid clubs. They are the result of a lot of research and development. What was learned is that most players tend to have difficulty hitting everything from their 6 iron down, basically all of their long irons. The natural tendency to want to hit it harder to get it farther caused people to veer from their normal swing. They were seldom able to hit the ball solidly and or take a divot. Seeing as the favored shot was taken with a sweeping motion, the hybrid was developed to accommodate that swing. The advantage of the hybrid is that you can hit the ball a long way without trying to kill the ball. They are designed to fill the gap between the mid-irons, and the fairway woods. They're also designed to assist in getting the ball up higher and easier. That's because they have more mass than the typical irons, and a lower center of gravity. Also, they don't require a divot. Another advantage is that you can get the head of the club through higher grass much easier, making it ideal for a rescue club. That's why they are quickly becoming the club of choice. So you can see that there are a lot of benefits with using a hybrid club. People with slower swing speeds can still hit it a great distance and maintain control of their shots. The main thing to remember if you want to have success with hybrids, is to stay behind the ball and don't over swing. Avoid swaying and keep the arms relaxed throughout the whole swing. You can even make a slight hesitation at the top of the swing. This will assist in keeping the tempo. If you haven't given them a try, I suggest that you consult a club fitter and have them introduce you to the newest thing.

BALANCE DRILLS

One thing that people usually struggle with is good balance. Here are a couple drills that will help. Take a wooden two-by-four, place it on the ground and put one foot in front of the other while taking a few swings.

Once you get comfortable hitting this way, switch your feet around and take a few more swings. This will force you to stay balanced.

Another drill that is beneficial for your swing is to hit balls with your feet together. For some people, however it's not as easy as it looks.

Just like the last drill, it also forces you to maintain balance and stay within your swing. If you lean too far in any direction, you will feel as though you are falling over. Balance is essential when putting your body into motion: Weight shift and good posture also rely upon it. In the swing, your weight moves in the direction of the club, and you should be conscious of where your weight is at all times. Good balance allows this to happen.

Something else to think about is that when the body is properly balanced, it uses far less energy while performing the swing; this greatly enhances one's endurance.

TENSION

Something you need to remember is tension in the swing; kills the swing. If you are too tense because you're trying to muscle up and hit the ball a long way, not only will you inhibit the swing from being performed correctly, you will actually cost yourself a great deal of distance. Too much tension will keep you from executing a smooth and complete release. You need to be loose and fluid when swinging the club. Fuzzy Zoeller, once made a comment that you need to feel as though there's oil in your veins. It's actually quite easy to remove tension from your body.

Something you can do to remove tension is to hold your club in the vertical position with your normal grip. When doing this the club will feel weightless. This is a static position.

As you bring the club down to the horizontal position, you will feel the full weight of the club, and at the same time, you'll feel your arms start to tighten up.

From this point, simply raise the club up to about a forty-five degree angle.

The weight should start to go away; then make circles with the clubhead. This will keep you aware of the weight at the end of the club and eliminate the tension.

PRACTICING WITH PURPOSE

As with any venture or desired task, the person needs to acquire all relevant information pertaining to it, learn how to perform it, and then spend time practicing it. Knowledge is essential if one wants to achieve success; however, spending time developing the necessary physical skills through repetitive actions, is what allows this to happen. Having a plan that continuously challenges the person's skill level or talent status promotes growth, and the ability for individuals to reach new levels. When the person spends time improving themselves with this thought in mind, they are practicing with purpose.

Going to the range and spending countless hours hitting balls with no specific goal in mind is not only non-productive, but will tend to ingrain poor habits and avoid the thinking process. Remember, practice isn't a matter of doing time, or torturing oneself by hitting a certain number of balls, then calling it quits. Practicing with purpose is having a specific goal in mind, knowing what you want to accomplish, and then having a plan to get there.

You may be experiencing a problem with distance, weight transfer, difficulty striking the ball cleanly, or any other part of your game. Where an all around game is needed, time and focus should be spent working on the areas that suffer most. The majority of players struggle with their short game, being 50 yards and in because this is where they tend to spend the least amount of time practicing. This is the part of the game that requires finesse, which tends to get rusty the quickest. Remember, golf is delegated through the mind, and performed through the body. It relies on feel, touch, trust, and commitment, which is why the pre-shot routine is so important.

As mentioned in the Pre-Shot Routine chapter of this book, some people tend to arrive at the course with little or no range time, and head out to the course to begin their round. When they start scattering shots all over the place, out comes the ole cliché. "Gee Wiz," I was striking the ball so nice on the range, but now I can't even hit it. What they fail to realize is they are actually playing two different games. In other words, when on the range, they will hit a shot, pull another ball from the pile and hit it, and the process continues. This is all done while standing in one spot. Keep in mind, there is no thought occurring during this process.

If the outcome is less than favorable, the thought is, oh well, I'll just hit another. There is no pressure or consequence involved in these shots; therefore the practice has no purpose.

When a player gets on the course, their mindset changes, and suddenly they feel pressure, realizing every shot counts. What they fail to realize; however, is time spent practicing on the range is a rehearsal of what they will be doing on the course. Another problem players' face is prior to taking each shot, they take several fluid practice swings, but when addressing the actual ball their mindset tends to change.

Panic is being placed in, or faced with an unfamiliar situation that offers significant consequences for poor performance. This is usually the result of a players' lack of confidence. The greater the consequence, the more intense the fear will become. If you take the time to practice with purpose you will not only boost your confidence but also learn to cope with the unknown, thus avoiding fear, and panic. The simple steps in practicing with purpose are, properly stretching prior to swinging the club, building a routine that emulates the conditions of the course, going through the pre-shot routine on every shot and sticking to the routine by taking the exact same steps every time which creates what is known as a comfort zone. It is extremely important to individualize a pre-shot routine, which can consist of any thoughts or actions, as long as it is consistent. This simply means: stand behind the ball in the same spot, go through the exact same thought process, and go through your personal checklist. The checklist is simply a list of things that you need to remember in the shot. Again, this was covered in the Pre-Shot routine chapter of this book. However, this is a great time to go through it again.

The process all begins from the think box and any problems you need to overcome or compensate for should be considered at this time and position. I go through a series of steps and thoughts prior to all of my shots, which I do exactly the same each and every time at my practice sessions as well as on the course. I stand behind the ball with my toes positioned exactly seven feet from the ball. I have my weight on my right foot and take a couple slow and deep breaths to ensure that my body is completely relaxed. My club is in the last three fingers of my left hand, which actually starts the grip. At this point, I gather all relevant information that could potentially affect the outcome of my shot. This would include alignment, elements like the wind or elevation, whether or not the ground is dry or wet, any hazards or obstacles that may come into play, and so on. Once I have taken everything into consideration, I decide my best option, commit to the shot, then I go through the same steps every time. Once I address the ball, I waggle twice, then, I pull the trigger. No second thoughts! It's all about doing the same thing exactly the same way every time. Going through these habitual and familiar steps will place you in your comfort zone, which will result in being consistent with what was done on the practice range.

It is also important to continuously change clubs and aim for different targets throughout your practice routine. There will be times when you are working on one specific shot with one particular club; however in general, rotating clubs during practice is most beneficial. If you spend too much time with one club, you will tend to stop the thought process needed to evaluate different situations in successfully navigating the course. After warming up, pick individual targets on the practice facility that might mimic the conditions of the course. This is done by hitting a driver, then an iron shot, and perhaps a chip shot; then, go through the process again. This type of practice will reveal weaknesses as well as keep the thought process going. It also maintains the feeling of going from an aggressive shot to an easy finesse shot. This will definitely pay huge dividends in your quest for lower scores. That is how you practice with purpose. Set goals, have a plan on how you want to accomplish them, and it is then that you will continue to grow.

ONE HANDED SWING DRILL

I've saved the best drill for last. All though it is quite simple to perform, the benefits are incredible. This is because several facets of the drill duplicate actual motions in the swing. I'm referring to a one handed swing, using only the forward or dominant hand, which is the hand closest to the intended target. It is important to remember that the swing is controlled by the forward side, and by allowing the rear hand to become dominant in the swing, it will only lead to hitting the ground behind the ball which known as a fat shot. When looking at the first two photos, you will notice that while I am swinging the club back and forth, my hips are rigid and my body isn't rotating at all.

When swinging this way, the club will feel very heavy and hard to control. The best way to perform this drill is to swing the club back and forth, striking the ground forward of center simulating a divot. As you continue swinging, begin rotating the body in the direction of the swing insuring that the hand and club are also fully rotating. As you can see in the next two photos, the toe of the club is now facing upward at each end, and the club is in front of my body at all times.

Lastly, your weight should shift in the direction of the swing. When doing this, you will notice that the weight of the club will tend to disappear, rendering the club weightless. This sensation will reveal how the club should feel during a normal swing. When both hands are on the club, however, it is easy to lose this feel without even knowing it, because the rear hand is stronger and it tends to override the control of the forward hand. It is important to swing the club at the same pace in both directions and have one side mirror the other. If you swing the club to the ten o'clock position, finish the swing at the two o'clock position. Focus on relaxing the body and try to feel pendulous with the swings. Doing this will synchronize the moving parts in the swing and help acquire the trust needed to hit crisp clean shots. It will also promote a balanced turn, thus leading to an effortless swing.

HOW TO BUY NEW EQUIPMENT AND WHAT TO LOOK FOR

I am always being asked by my new students as to the type and brand of equipment they should purchase. My advice to them is not to run out, and spend a lot of money buying new clubs while in the learning process. This is due to the fact that a consistent swing has not been established, and will result in an improper fitting. I recommend starting out with a used set of clubs, which can be fairly inexpensive and easily adjusted to fit any player. Club fitters have the equipment to make any necessary adjustments.

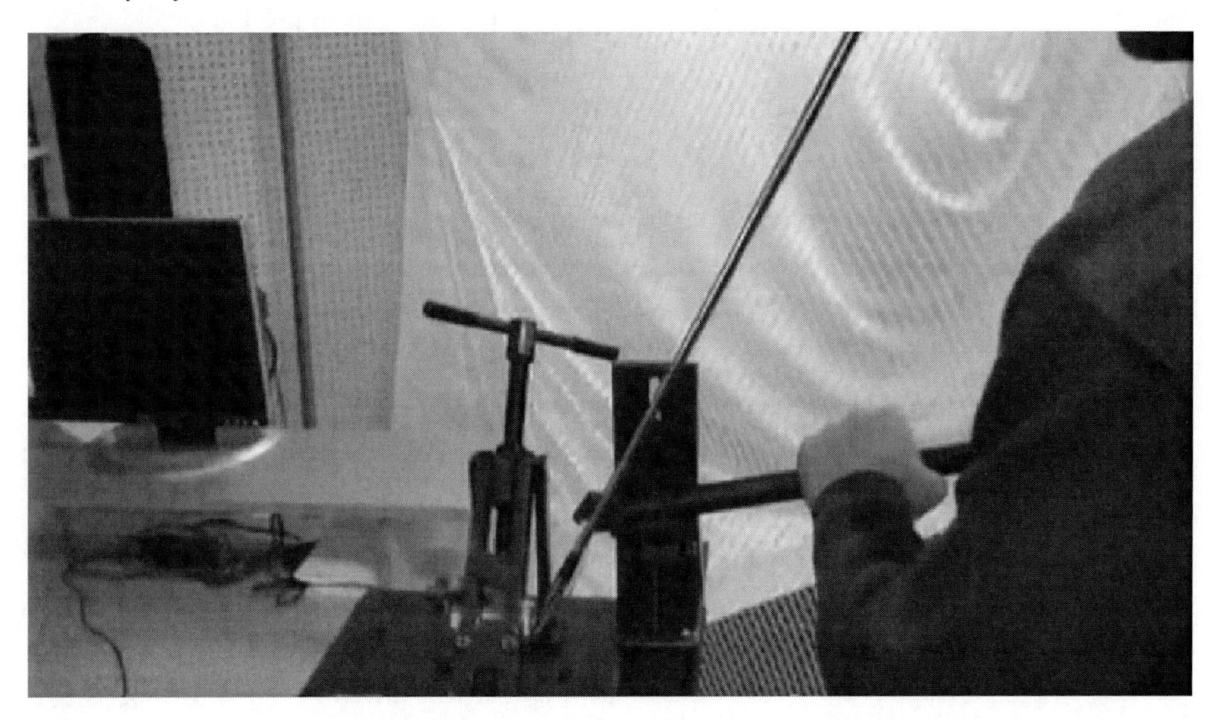

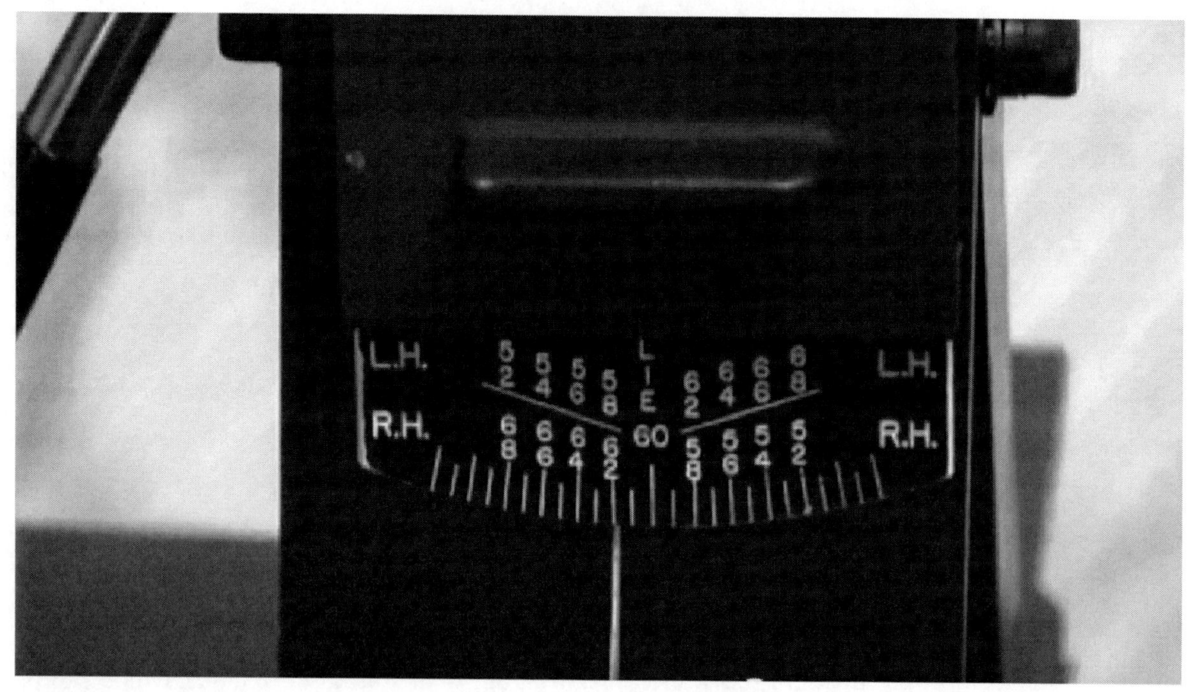

Once a consistent swing has been developed, and the ball is being struck cleanly, it is then that they should consider going to a professional to have clubs fitted. This will avoid the need to purchase clubs multiple times. After you reach this point, the next part of this book will help you understand the process of club selection.

CLUB SELECTION—WHAT TO LOOK FOR?

Buying a set of clubs isn't something to take lightly. It can be a large investment, but more important, it can determine your ability to perform properly, and achieve great golf shots. If done incorrectly, it can limit one's ability to improve or reach goals, which can lead to confusion and frustration. Understanding your equipment, along with knowing how it is designed to function will help in knowing what to ask for when getting fitted for clubs. It is extremely important that the player have a consistent and repeating swing in order to achieve proper measurements. The following factors need to be taken into consideration when being fitted for clubs.

CLUB LENGTH

The length of the club shaft is typically determined by taking into consideration, a player's height, the type of club they are using, and the angle the club will lie at address. When a player has good posture, the correct length can be assessed. The shaft length will vary with the wedges being the shortest, and the driver being the longest. This will affect the total width of the swing, as well as the clubhead speed.

LIE ANGLE

The lie angle is the angle that the club leans toward the player at address, relative to the ground. It is the measurement of degrees between the centerline of the hosel, and the sole of the clubhead, when the sole is touching the ground at the center of the clubhead. The lie angle is acquired by taking a strip of marking or masking tape, placing it along the sole of the club, then placing a ball on the surface, and striking it with a normal swing.

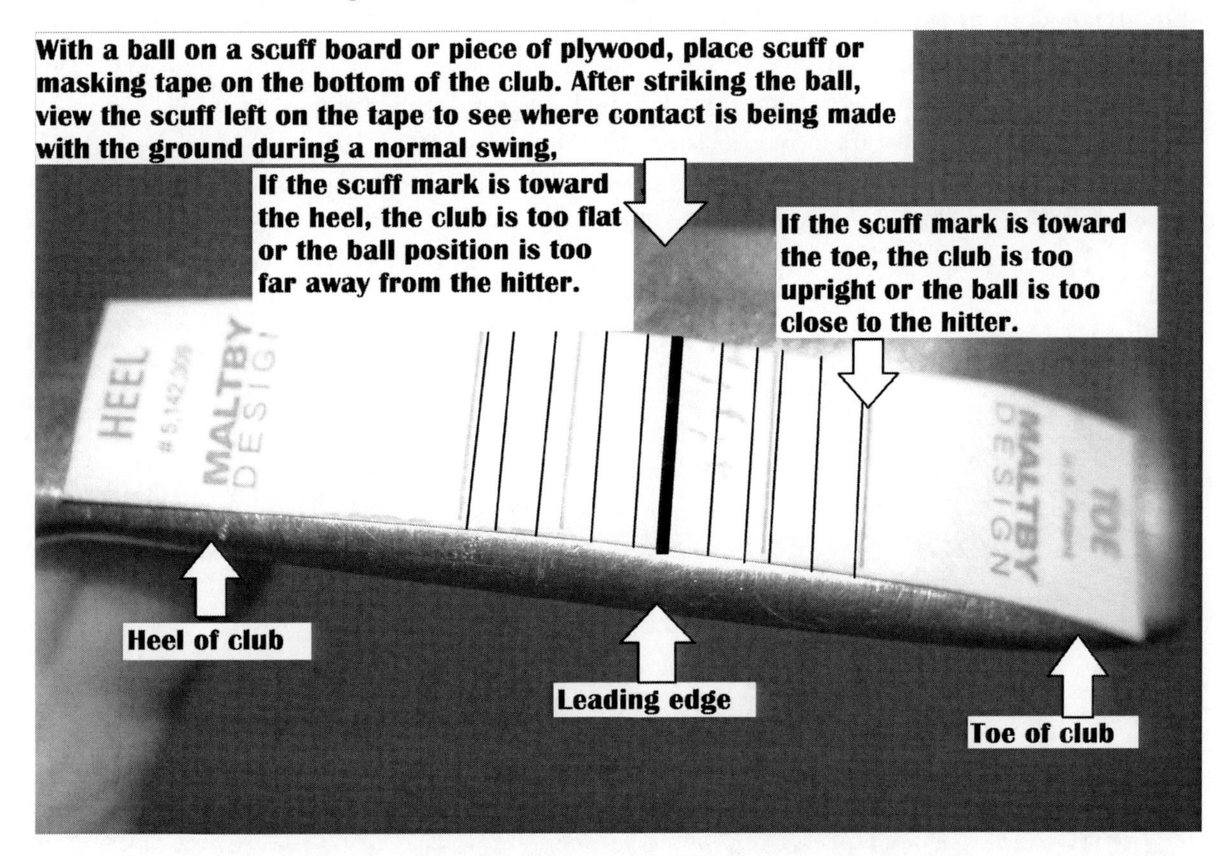

The tape indicates the point of contact by revealing a scuff mark where the bottom of the clubhead made contact with the ground. However, depending on the flexibility of the shaft, the club can indicate a different point of contact during a swing as opposed to the still address position. This takes us to the next item.

TOE DEFLECTION

During the swing, the toe of the club will move down, toward the ground, as a result of the centrifugal force placed on the shaft. The faster the swing, the more influence it will have on the deflection. As the shaft bends back and forth, it also bends down. Most golfers extend their arms through impact, causing their hands to rise during the downswing, and the toe of the club will go down. This can greatly influence the direction that the ball travels off of the face of the club.

THE SHAFT

The preferred shaft material for woods is graphite, whereas steel is typically favored for irons. Graphite and composite shafts continue to increase in popularity, especially as technology in graphite allows it to perform as good as, or even better than steel. Graphite has several benefits, such as being lighter, easier to swing and softer during impact which dampens the vibration. It also has an added advantage of being more versatile, which helps in fitting a wide range of golfers. Steel, on the other hand, is by nature more consistent. Stronger players generally prefer steel shafts with their irons, because they can apply more torque to the club without losing control or experiencing too much flex in the shaft.

SHAFT FLEX

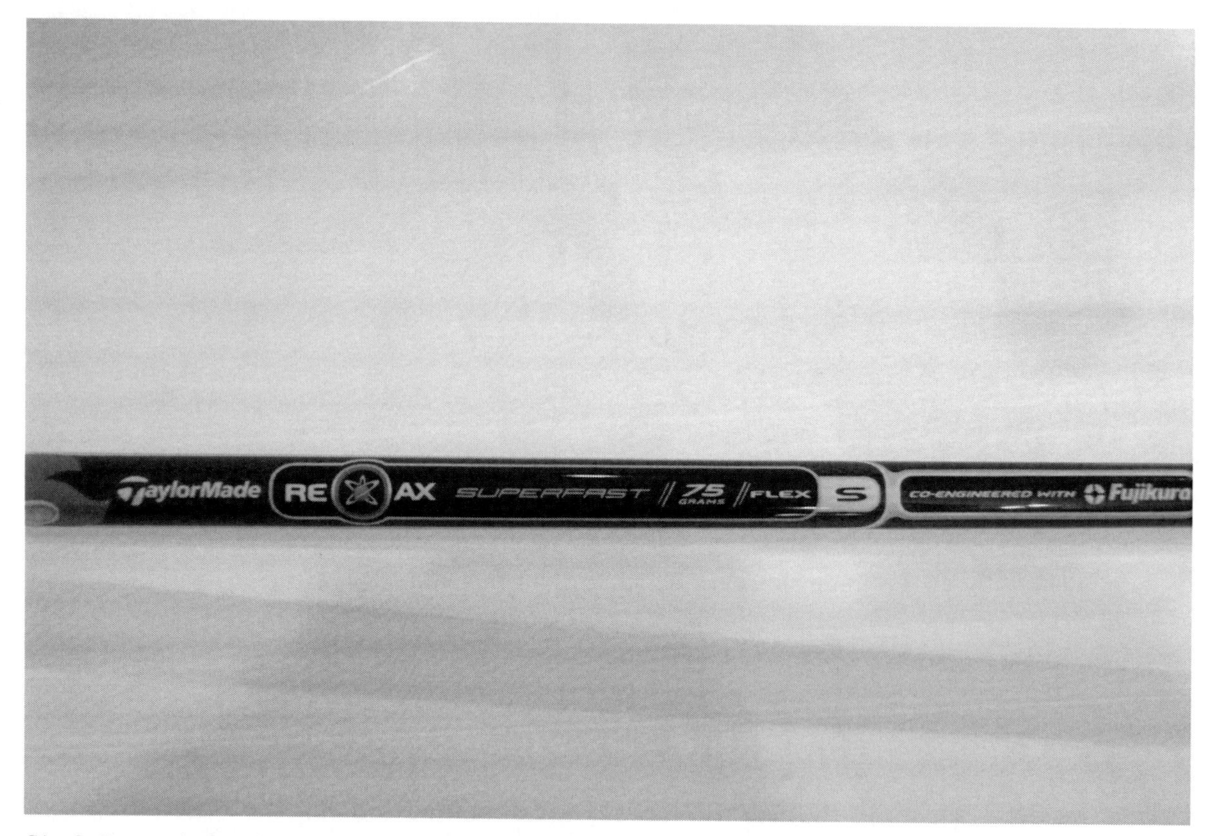

Shaft flex is defined as how much the shaft bends or gives in a back and forth manner.

The flex designation printed on the shaft only pertains to that particular shaft model. What is stiff to one model may not be stiff to another. Due to this fact, the first step in choosing a proper shaft should be to choose the type and model prior to considering the flex itself.

TORSIONAL STIFFNESS (TORQUE)

Torsional stiffness is simply the amount of twist that a shaft will experience when being swung by a golfer. A composite or graphite shaft will typically twist more than a steel shaft. There are, however, some composite shafts, which are tighter woven and have less torsional stiffness than steel. The lower the rating, the lower the amount of twisting when put under stress. These are typically your higher grade and more expensive shafts.

FLEX POINT

The flex point, also referred to as the kick point, is where the most bending occurs on the shaft.

This is a factor which has an impact on the trajectory of the ball. The lower the flex point, the higher the ball flight. Keep in mind, the flex points of different shafts only vary slightly.

FREQUENCY ANALYZING

Frequency analyzing is measuring the flex of a shaft by using a computer called a frequency analyzer. The shaft is rated by the computer according to cycles per minute of revolution. This process is significantly more accurate when testing shafts, as opposed to the deflection board method relied upon for many years. The main benefit of this is to ensure that the shafts in a set of clubs are synchronized, thus producing a consistent feel and reaction throughout the set.

HEAD DESIGN

The clubhead design has a significant effect when striking the ball, as well as the flight. It can also influence the level of confidence a player has. It is important that you place a higher value on the shaft than the clubhead when selecting clubs. When buying woods, there are a number of significant factors that must be taken into consideration. They are: face angle, vertical roll, head size (usually measured by cubic centimeters), face bulge, center of gravity, and the thickness of the face wall.

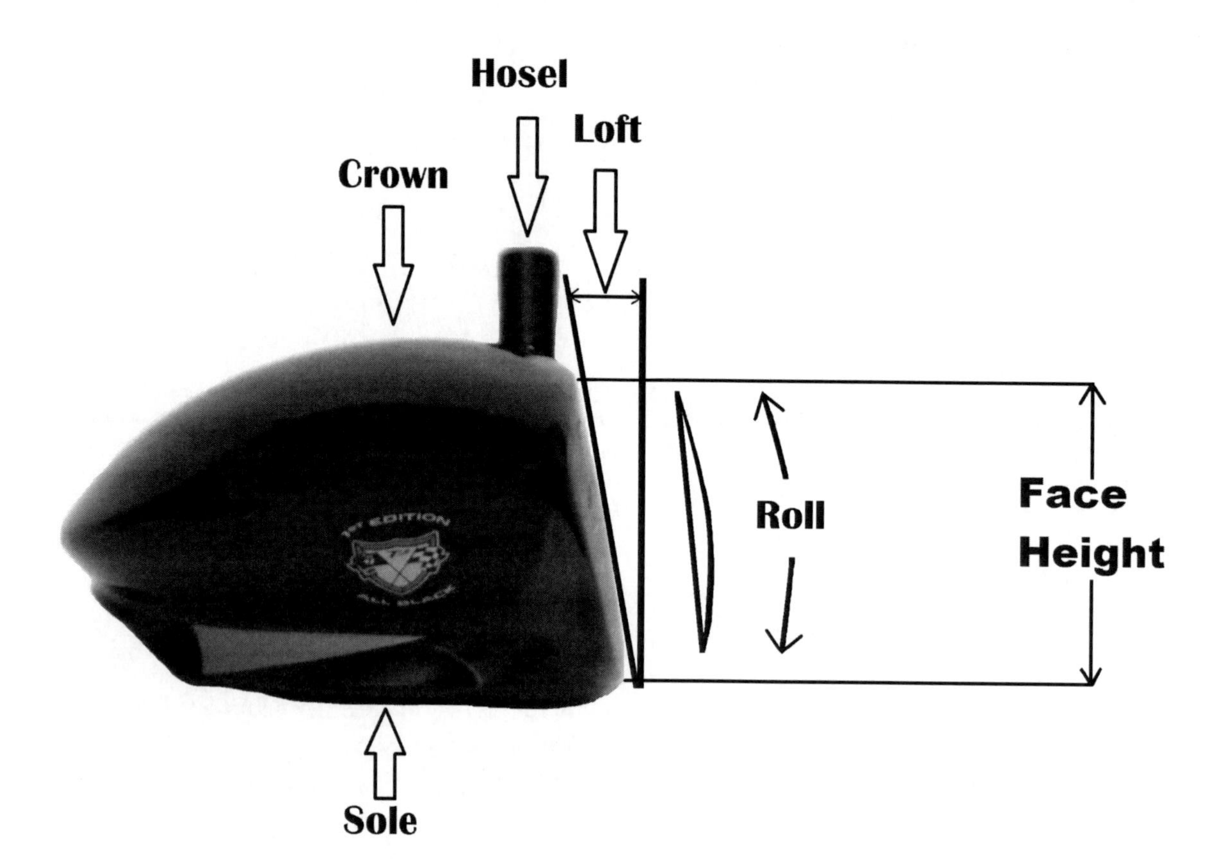

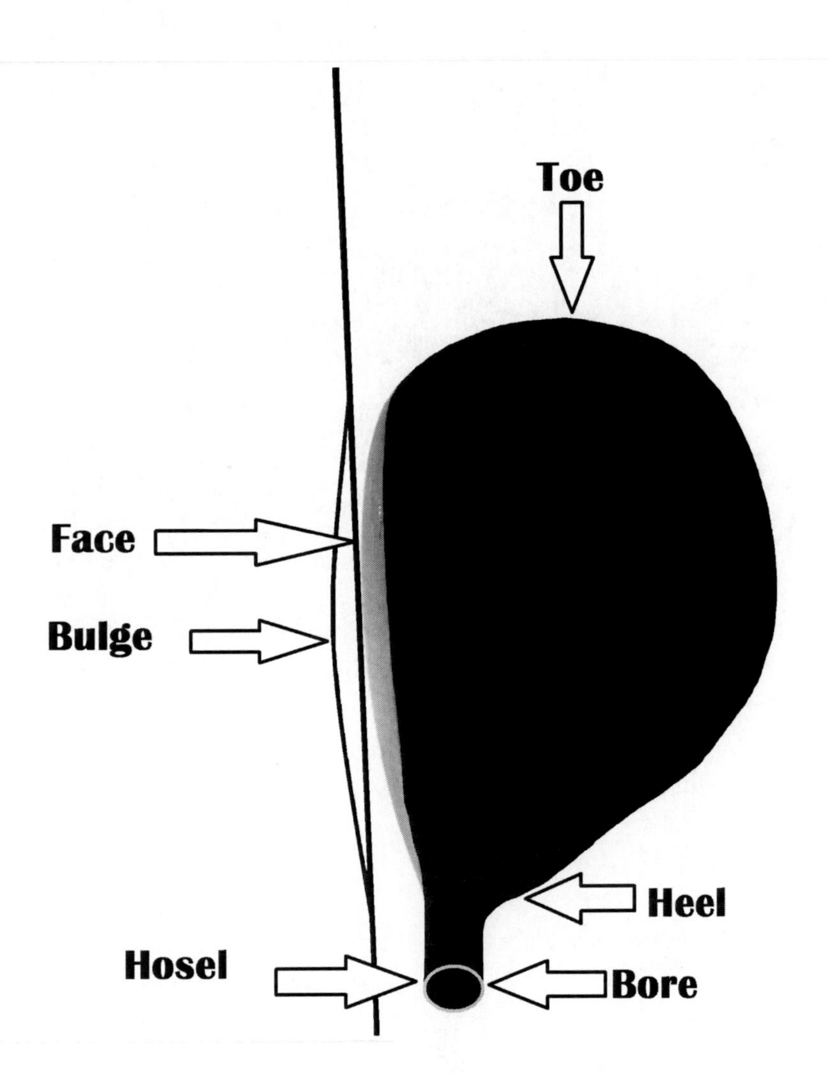
Toe
Face
Bulge
Heel
Hosel
Bore

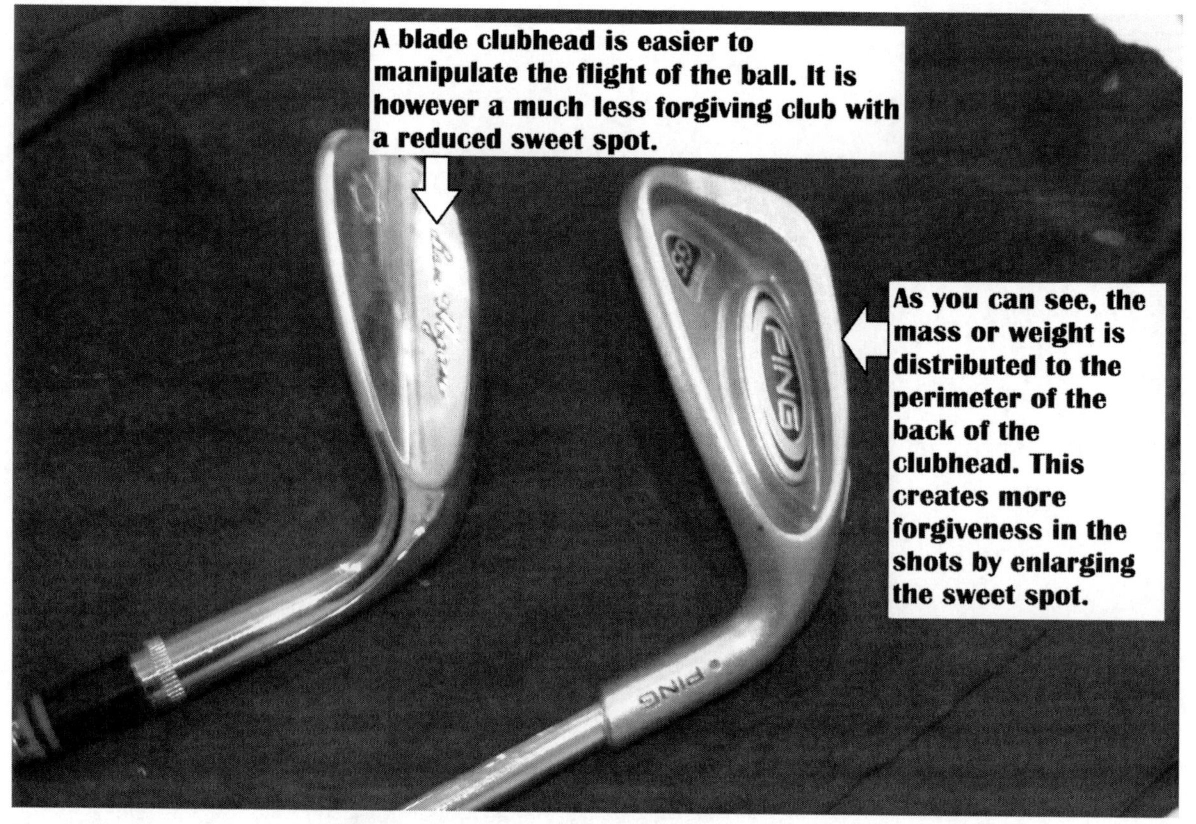

These factors can greatly influence the trajectory despite the loft of the club. Loft is easy to see; however, the other factors must be taken into consideration in understanding the effect on ball flight. While head size can affect center of gravity, different manufacturers place inserts into the clubhead for reinforcement, which will affect the location of the center of gravity, as well.

LOFT

Loft is simply the angle measured in degrees between the vertical or upright plane of the clubface and the centerline of the hosel. The term strong and weak refers to the loft of a club versus the standard loft typically used by manufacturers for a club. If a club is considered to be in a strong position, it will be in a less lofted angle producing a lower trajectory flight. If the club is considered to be in a weak position, it will be at a more lofted angle. Loft standards can vary from one manufacturer to another. A true understanding of loft requires understanding its relationship with clubhead speed. The faster the clubhead travels, the more the ball rolls up the face of the club, thus launching the ball higher. There are several factors that influence trajectory. They are center of gravity, loft of the club and with the woods, the face angle and offset angle of attack. Ball flight laws will come into play based on the face position at impact relative to the swing path.

GRIP

Grip size is determined by the diameter of the core, and the butt of the club, which can be found in a wide variety of material, based on preference.

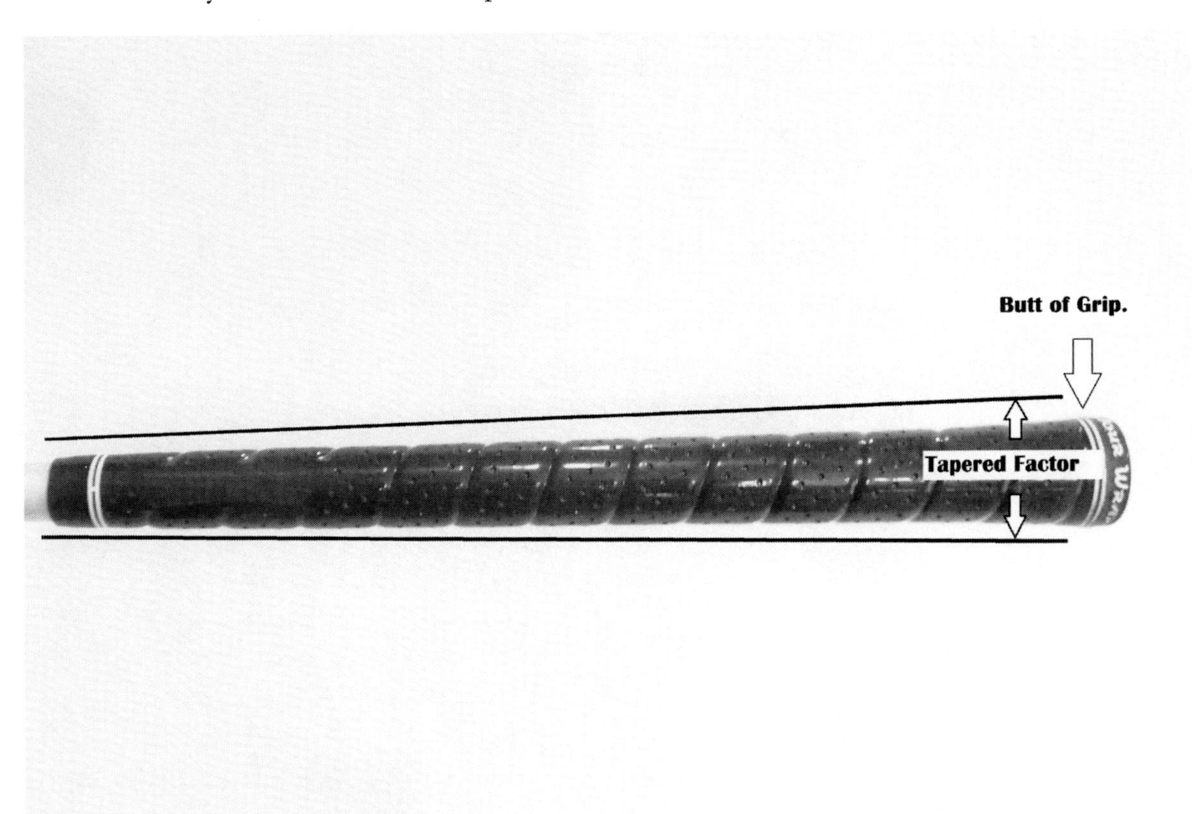

When getting correctly fitted for grips they must be comfortable in the hands. This allows the golfer to grip the club loosely, without the feeling of it slipping away, thus avoiding tension in the arms. Tension tends to lead to an early release. The fingertips should comfortably touch the inner palm of the hand at the base of the thumb as it wraps around the grip. Clubs are designed with what's referred to as a tapered factor where the extreme butt of the grip is flared to alleviate the need to hold on tight. Centrifugal force in the swing actually pulls the club tighter into the hands so the hitter does not feel the need to choke the club to keep from losing it.

FACE ANGLE

Face angle is the angle in degrees between the face of the club and the target line, when the hosel is considered square to the target line. Face angle is usually determined in the fairway woods and the driver. They will either be open, square, or closed. Advanced players tend to use the visual effect of the clubhead at address to align their shots and visualize the ball flight.

STATIC WEIGHT

Static weight is merely the actual weight of the club, and usually measured in ounces. Advanced players and people with faster swings generally favor a heavier club. These are player's that properly use their body to produce the swing; whereas, a person with a slower swing will favor a lighter club due to the fact that they tend to use their arms more than they should.

MAINTAINING EQUIPMENT

Golf enthusiasts spend a lot of time and money working on all aspects of their game. This is all in an effort to produce admirable scores out on the golf course. Many individuals even invest in lessons to improve their mechanics and fundamentals. Then they lay out even more money for memberships and green fees. All in all, golf can be an expensive sport.

I am surprised at the fact that with so much on the line, they fail to maintain the most important detail, "their equipment." After practicing and/or playing the course, being done for the day they just throw their clubs in the trunk of their car,

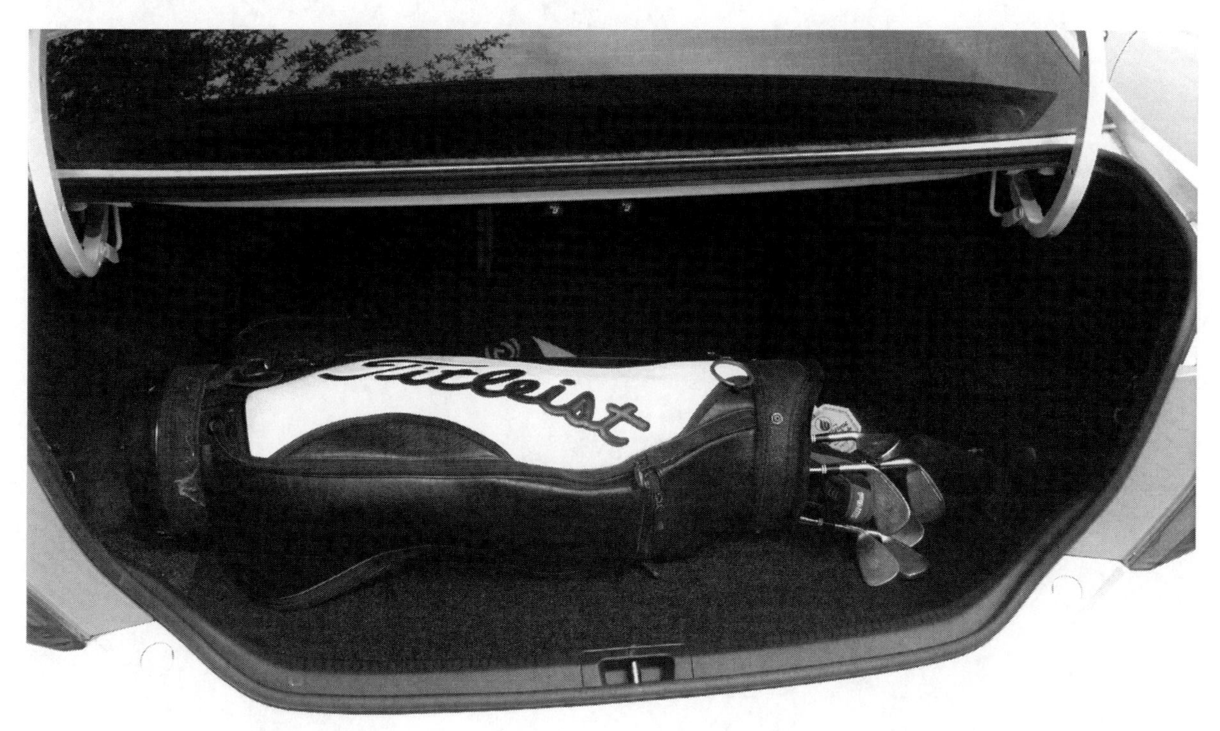

and go on about their normal business. The next time they go to use their equipment they pull them out and go. What mystifies me is that they wonder why the clubs fail to perform at their potential, yet they never take the time to clean or maintain them.

Golf clubs are like an automobile. If you don't maintain them, they reach a point where they fail to perform as they were designed. The irons have grooves in the face, designed to control the flight of the ball;

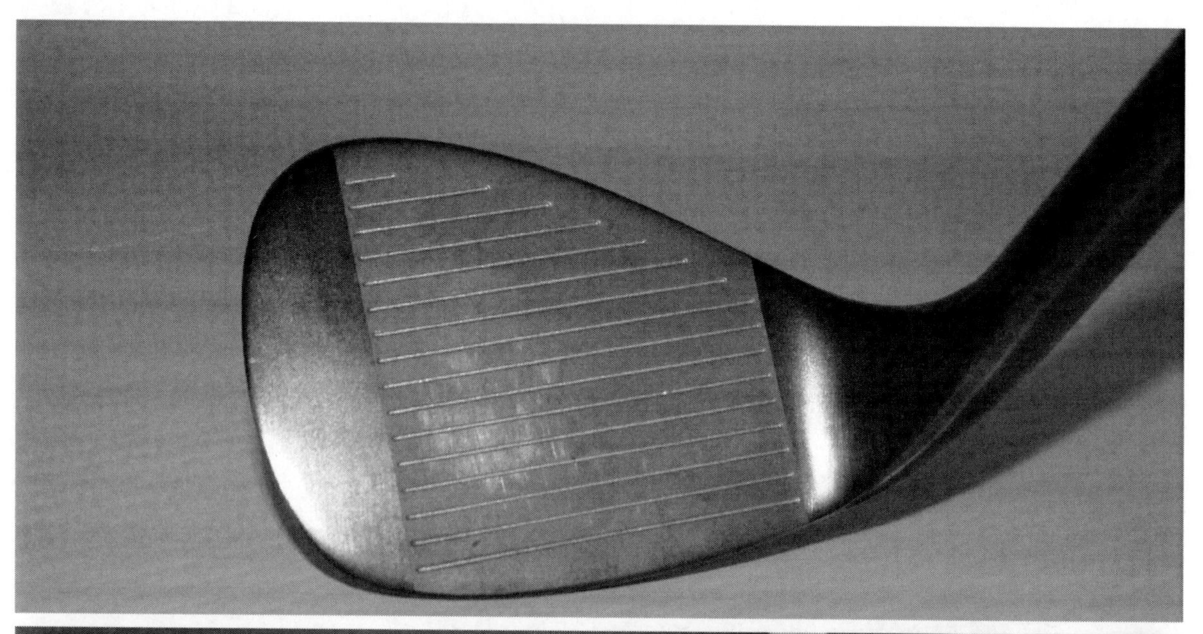

Keeping the grooves of the clubs clean will allow them to do what they were designed to do.

Something else many players fail to realize or consider is when golf clubs are left in a vehicle for a duration of time, and exposed to extreme temperatures, they are adversely affected. It can change the lie angles of the irons, speed up the deterioration of the grips, and break down the fibers in the graphite, which greatly diminishes the integrity of the material, and hinders its ability to perform correctly. I highly encourage players to protect their investment by taking the time to maintain and care for their equipment after each use, which includes proper storage when not in use.

How many times have you left a club at a previously played hole only to realize at the time it's needed, it's missing? We've all experienced that heart-stopping drama. A simple method that I have found to avoid this from happening is to place the head cover in your pocket after removing it from the club being used.

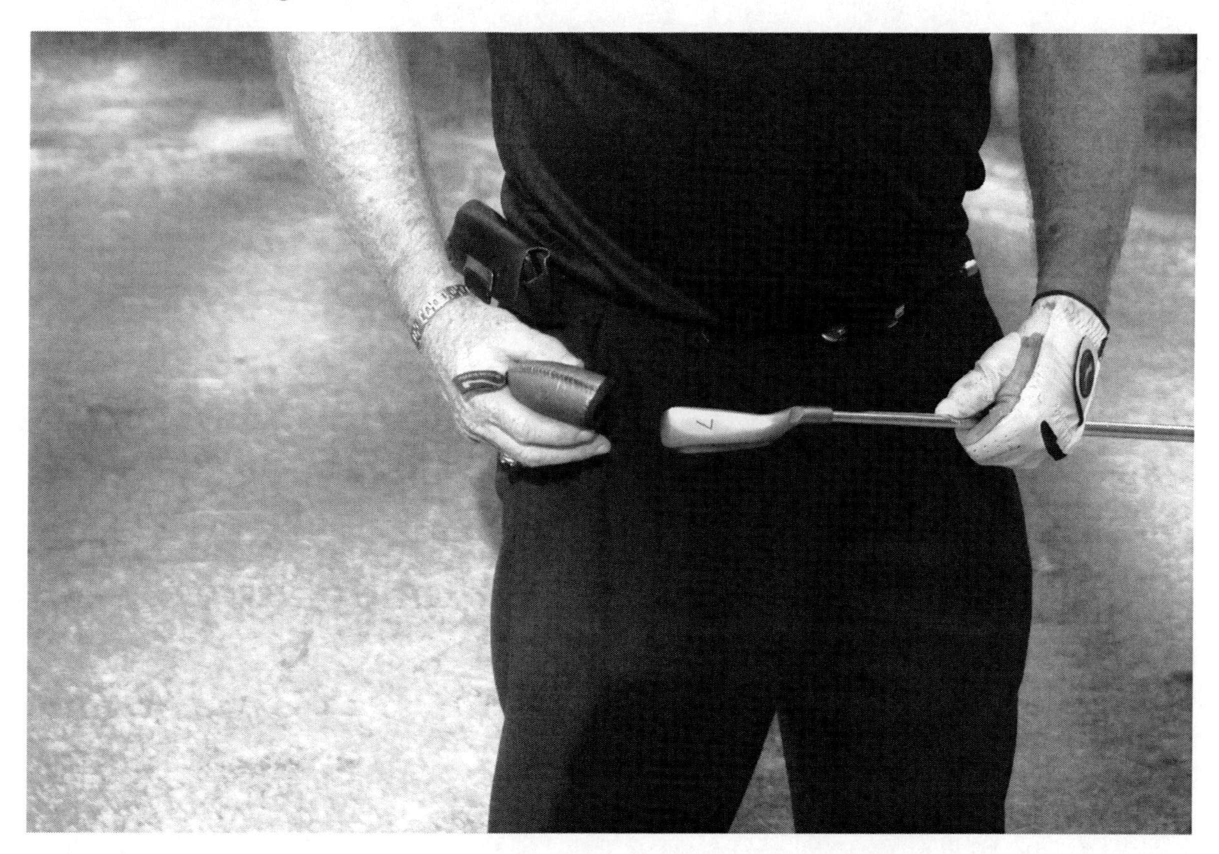

After taking each shot I immediately put the head cover back on and return it to my bag. If at any time, I feel a head cover in my pocket I know a club is missing. This is a great habit to develop and a good way to keep from leaving a club behind. Some golf bags have individual compartments for each club for easy access. It is a great idea to take the time and organize the clubs in a particular order, preferably numerically, so when you see an empty space, you can easily identify the missing club. This has saved me numerous times, especially when taking multiple clubs to the green.

Hole	1	2	3	4	5	6	7	8	9	Out	INITIAL	10	11	12	13	14	15	16	17	18	In	Tot	Hcp	Net
Yellow 72.5/124	526	394	196	409	117	424	387	375	547	3375		434	422	174	395	509	425	403	199	571	3532	6907		
Blue 71.8/123	507	384	141	400	105	392	375	368	535	3207		412	381	154	374	497	415	389	184	557	3363	6570		
White 69.3/121	480	360	135	372	95	366	330	345	517	3000		385	360	138	353	476	397	372	166	534	3181	6181		
Handicap	9	13	11	1	17	3	15	7	5			4	10	16	18	14	12	8	6	2				
John Doe	6	4	4	4	4	4	4	5	5	40		4	4	3	3	5	4	4	4	5	36	76		
Fairways		✓	X	✓	X	✓	✓		✓	5		✓	✓	X	✓	✓		✓	X	✓	6	11		
GREENS		✓	B	C	C	B C	✓	B	C	2		✓	C	✓	✓	B	C	✓	B	C	4	6		
Par	5	4	3	4	3	4	4	4	5	36		4	4	3	4	5	4	4	3	5	36	72		
PUTTS	2	2	2	1	2	1	2	2	2	16		2	2	2	1	1	1	2	2	2	15	31		
BUNKERS			1			1		1		3						1			1		2	5		
Red 71.5/125	434	318	116	350	80	302	305	307	442	2654		348	301	138	308	452	330	325	132	494	2828	5482		

Date: Scorer: self Score Attest:

Keep statistics of your round of golf each time you play on a score card as shown here. This will reveal where you need improvement in your game and will assist in practicing with purpose. As you improve, your statistics will show it. I enter (B) for bunkers and (C) for when I chipped the ball.

POWER

Power is one of the most highly used words in golf. It's also one of the most misunderstood words as well. In general, people tend to think of power as brute strength, able to apply great force to an object in an attempt to move it. In golf however, power is referred to in the form of technique. If you're wondering what I'm talking about, look at some of the longest hitters on tour. They're not particularly muscular. They have mastered the ability to combine their body movements in a way that has them all work together and combine their force. In essence, the movements are synchronized. With that, one is able to apply the forces of nature referred to as leverage, which will either work against you or with you. The ideal thing is to use them to your advantage. Any time there is a hinge or turn in a moving object, there is a lever involved. In a golf swing, there's several hinges involved. I'm sure at this time that you're probably wondering what I'm talking about. Well, I'll explain.

We'll pretend that the end of my fingertips is the head of the club. The ultimate goal is to achieve a high rate of speed. After all, that's how we get greater distance, right? We'll start with the first lever, the shoulder. If I move my arm up and down in a particular motion, I will achieve a certain speed at the end of the object. If I do the same thing with the elbow only, it will give the same general results. If I combine the two levers together, notice how much faster the finger tips are moving. Now if we add the wrists as a third lever, we add additional speed. The combining of these levers is referred to as compounded levers. In the golf swing however, there are additional levers involved. If you've ever been to a carnival or county fair, somewhere that has rides, you will probably recall some of the rides that have several turning points simultaneously. It's a ride that will give you a feeling of a slingshot. This is where the hips come in. We like to think of the hips as an accumulator as well as an accelerator. It takes a moving object, and multiplies it's speed in the same direction. Now you've really got a great amount of movement. This all works to your advantage as long as the levers are aligned in the same direction. That is where the swing plane comes in to play and why it's so important. If you were going to grab a hammer and drive a nail into a board, you would get your best results if the arm, wrist, and the hammer are all in alignment. If you turn your wrist in one direction or the other, you will significantly reduce your power, leverage and even if you swing the hammer at the same rate of speed, the results will be much less effective. These are simple movements to achieve however, they are crucial to getting the desired results. It's not something that you need to bog yourself down with, it's just important that you understand their significance and how they come into play.

CUSTOMIZING A GOLF LESSON

For generations, it has been thought that in order to acquire a great golf swing and to expect favorable results, one must fit the mold that has been created which we consider to be the ideal swing. Though it is true that one must adhere to the basic elements, we must remember that a particular swing doesn't work the same for every individual. Due to unique characteristics of each person, each student is like a fingerprint. From a distance, we are all generally the same. However, upon closer observation, no two people are exactly the same. My point in this is that although certain body movements are necessary to guide the club in a particular way, resulting in achieving a favorable ball strike, several important things have to be taken into consideration. Where one individual may be young, healthy, and flexible, others may have certain physical limitations. Where proper rotation, weight shift, shoulder turn and a wide arc may come easy to some, others would find it to be difficult or even impossible to perform. This can be from prior surgery, a bad back, age, or any other reason.

Customizing a swing for any individual is truly an art. By interviewing the student and getting some history on them as well as asking them what they are hoping to achieve, you can gain a lot of information about their true knowledge of the game based on their expression and verbiage. This gives you a great starting point as well as the opportunity to build a strategy that will best suit them and their needs. This includes not only the speed that you could expect to move along, but the amount of information that you feel they could handle at one time. Gathering important knowledge about the student is like a pre-shot routine. It allows you to focus on what you are about to do and put in into perspective.

At this point, it's time to observe a practice swing, explain a few basic elements, then place a ball in front of them and observe the flight. This will give you a great starting point. Based on the results of several shots, it can be determined if there is a consistency in the results and allow you to point out minor changes. It will also convey their receptiveness to new information as well as their ability to follow instructions. This is important to know if you have any hopes of achieving favorable results. After suggesting small changes, it is important to explain what you are doing so they won't feel as though you are using them as a test of your own uncertainty. It will also build great confidence in their view of you. They will be much more willing to try something that you suggest, even though it may feel unnatural or awkward. The student must always feel that their best interest is your main concern and not your pride or image as an expert. They will be more apt to put their heart into their efforts which will help achieve the results that you were striving for. Remember, it is important to recognize that if someone fails to attain the desired results, it might be best to remove that thought and try something else. At all cost, remind the student that it is not a sign of failure on their part, it is simply a vital step in searching for what works best for them. From there, using what you have observed and gathered, build a strategy that will remain simplified and satisfying to the student. They will truly understand what your lesson was based on as well as what it was designed to achieve. With basic and uncomplicated drills, they will continue to grow and will know that their lesson with you was time well spent.

GLOSSARY

(A)

Ace: Another word for a hole-in-one.

Address Position: Taking a stance and placing the clubhead behind the ball in preparation for playing a shot.

Advice: Information given to another player during a stipulated round. This is anything other than general information known by the general public, such as distance to a hole, location of a hazard, etc.

Aim: The direction in which the player aligns for a shot, typically for a specific target or landing area.

Albatross: This is a term used when the score on a hole is "three-under-par." It's also known as a *Double Eagle.*

Alignment: The manner and direction in which a player aims to hit a shot, based on lines formed by the clubface, feet, knees, hips, and most importantly the shoulders.

A.G.A.: An acronym for "*American Golf Association.*"

Approach shot: Term used to describe a short shot onto the green from the fairway or rough.

Apron: This is the closely mowed area between the green and the surrounding area.

Arc: The path traveled by the clubhead during the swing.

Away: When playing in a group of two or more, the golfer whose ball is farthest from the hole is said to be "away." On all shots , it's customary for the golfer who is away to hit his shot first, followed by the player with the next-longest shot, and so on until the group has finished the hole. The exception to this is from the "tee box." The person who is said to have the honors, hits first from the "tee box." *See Honors*

(B)

Back Nine: The second set of nine holes on an 18 hole course.

Backspin: A term used when a golf ball rotates in the opposite direction of flight when set in motion. This is typically used to stop the golf ball quickly after in lands.

Backswing: The initial section of the swing in which the golfer pulls the club away from its position behind the ball. The backswing ends when the golfer begins his movement back toward the ball, starting the downswing.

Baseball Grip: A grip in which all ten fingers are placed on the grip of the club. Commonly referred to as the "ten finger grip."

Bare Lie: A term used when a ball is sitting in an area with little, or no grass.

Bias on a Golf Club: A clubhead that is weighted to produce a particular ball flight is said to have "bias."

Birdie: A score of one-under-par on a hole.

Blast: A shot from a bunker where the player strikes sand before the `ball, sending both into the air toward the target. Also referred to as, an "Explosion Shot."

Block: A straight shot that travels outward, relative to the target line. A "block" occurs when the golfer fails to properly release the hands through impact. Also referred to as, a "flare" or "push shot."

Bogey: A score of one-over-par on a hole.

Bounce: The wide rounded edge on the sole or bottom of the club, measured in degrees which varies between the leading and trailing edge. Usually referring to the sand wedge with 10-12 degrees being standard.

Break or Borrow: The degree or amount of curvature that a ball is affected by the slope or contour of the putting surface.

Bulge and Roll: The faces of woods are not uniformly flat, but slightly curved. The curvature from heel to toe (horizontal) is called bulge, while top to bottom (vertical) curvature is called roll.

Bump and Run: A low trajectory shot intended to get the ball rolling along the ground and onto the green, as opposed to flying onto the green. The bump-and-run is often used when the turf is firm and no hazards, or rough lie between the ball and the target.

Bunker: Also referred to as a "Sand Trap," consisting of sand, grass or both that exists as an obstacle and in some cases, a hazard. Specific rules govern play from these hazards.

(C)

Carry: A term used to describe the distance that a ball travels after being struck by a club.

Casting: Prematurely releasing the angle which is established between the forward arm and the club in the downswing.

Casual Water: A temporary accumulation of water on the course usually from rain or irrigation, and is not considered a water hazard; it's visible before or after the player takes his stance.

Cavity Back: This is a term used to describe the back side of a clubhead that is hollow in the center and solid around the perimeter. This is also referred to as Perimeter weighted. It is designed to be more forgiving, and tends to have a lower center of gravity, thus helping the ball into the air.

Centrifugal Force: The outward force of an object from the center, while rotating around an axis. The higher the speed the greater the force is.

Centripetal Force: The force that has to be applied directly opposite the centrifugal force. This is applied through the grip, as a form of resistance.

Chip Shot: This is a low running shot, usually played around the edge of the green when putting is not feasible. It is also known as a shot that rolls farther than it flies.

Choke: This is a common term used when a player loses his or her nerve and fails under pressure.

Choke Down: This term is used to describe shortening the club by placing the hands on the club toward the bottom of the grip.

Closed Stance: This is a term used to describe the body alignment relative to the target line or swing path. When more of the player's back is facing the target than the front, it is said to be in a "closed stance or position."

C.O.G.: An acronym for center of gravity. The point in a clubhead where all of the points of balance intersect. The lower the center of gravity, the higher the ball flight is. Higher center of gravity clubs produce lower ball flight.

C.O.M.: An acronym for center of mass. This is the stability produced by the equal distribution of weight on each side of a vertical axis. Center of mass is also referred to as center of balance.

Cut: This is a term used when a player fails to post a score which qualifies them to continue throughout a 72 hole tournament. The cut is usually established after 36 holes, and based on the average score of the field.

Cut Shot: A term used to describe a shot that produces a curvature of ball flight in the direction in front of the person hitting, which is also known as a slice. This produces a loftier shot. It may be accidental or deliberate.

(D)

Divot: This is the removal of ground surface or turf that is removed by the clubhead as a result of a downward hit after striking the ball. It doesn't influence the ball, it is only an indication that the ball was struck in a downward direction. A divot is highly encouraged with irons.

Dogleg: This is a term used to describe a hole layout that changes in either direction between the tee box and the green.

Dormie: A term used in Match Play when a player is leading in as many holes as there are left, and therefore, cannot be beaten.

Double Bogey: A score of two-over-par on a hole.

Double Eagle: A score of three-under-par on a hole, also known as an Albatross.

Downswing: The descending part of the swing where the clubhead is moving down, toward the ball.

Draw: A term used to describe a shot that produces ball flight that subtly curves in the direction behind the player, from right to left, for a right-handed player; and left to right, for a left-handed player. The term "Draw" also refers to the deciding factor in Match play, as to whom will have the honors, and go first.

Driver: This is a minimal lofted club designed to hit the ball off of a tee. It is swung in a slightly ascending direction producing the maximum distance down the fairway. It is also the longest club in the bag.

Duff: This is a slang word used when a player fails to execute a shot properly, resulting in a poor outcome.

(E)

Eagle: A score of two-under-par on a hole.

(F)

Fade: A term used to describe a shot that produces a ball flight that subtly curves in the direction in front of the player relative to the target line. For a right-handed player, this would be a left-to-right shot.

Fairway: This is the closely mowed area between the tee box and the green, designed to be a landing area on longer holes.

Fat Shot: A description of a shot when the clubhead strikes the ground behind the ball, resulting in poor contact and a shot that comes well short of the target.

Flex Point: Also referred to as the "Kick Point," where most of the bending occurs in the shaft. This is a factor which has an impact on the trajectory of the ball. The lower the flex point, the higher the ball flight. Keep in mind that the flex points of different shafts only vary slightly.

Flop Shot: This is a short and extremely lofty shot played with an open stance, a more horizontal swing path and an open clubface, designed to travel very high in the air on a steep trajectory and land softly on the green; thus minimizing the roll after it lands.

Fluffy Lie: Also known as a "perched lie." A lie in which the ball comes to rest atop the grass suspended above the ground.

Follow-Through: The part of the swing that occurs after the ball has been struck.

Fried Egg: The slang term for a buried lie in the sand of the bunker.

Four Ball: This is a term used in (match play), involving four players in teams of two, where each player plays their own ball.

Foresome: (1) A match that involves four players in teams of two, where each team plays one ball and alternates shots throughout the round, starting on the first hole. (2) A group of four players in a group, playing each hole, remaining together and playing each person's own ball and maintaining their own score, throughout the entire round.

Free Drop: The act of dropping a ball without penalty away from an immovable obstacle, or any other circumstances that are stipulated by the rules of golf.

Front Nine: The first nine holes on an 18 hole course.

(G)

Grain: The direction which the blades of grass grow, or influenced by the flow of water, which is of primary importance on the greens, as this can effect the movement of the ball.

Graphite Shaft: Graphite is a carbon fiber that is layered and bonded together to produce a strong, yet flexible material, ideal for golf shafts. Different weaves produce different flex points and overall flexibility. It is also used as a composite for some clubheads.

Green: The closely mown area where the flag and hole are located.

Grip: The grip is referred to as the area of a club which is designed for the hands to be placed when holding the club. There are multiple materials used which are designed to give the player comfort, and the thickness can vary, depending on the size of the player's hands. The term "grip" is also referred to as the act of placing the hands on the club.

Grounding the Club: This is a term used when the player allows the head of the club to touch the ground in a hazard. This is a violation of the rules.

GTAA: An acronym for, "*Golf Teachers' Academy of America.*"

(H)

Handicap: This is a system that subtracts strokes from less experienced players, designed to give everyone an equal chance during a competition. This is established by three things. (1) The tee box which the player is playing from, (2) The actual score that the player posts for their round, and (3) The index as well as slope rating of the course. It is measured in + or – numbers, depending on the ability of the player and derived by using an average score over time.

Hazard: This is an area, other than the closely mowed fairway designated for regulation play. This term is also used when referring to a bunker or sand trap.

Heel: The part of the clubhead nearest the hosel.

Hole: The hole, measuring 4.25 in. (10.8cm) in diameter, also referred to as the (bottom of the cup), which is marked with a pin or flagstick. This is the point in which the ball must come to rest in order to consider the hole completed, prior to proceeding to the next teeing ground.

Honors: The player who is to play first from the teeing ground is said to have the "Honor." This is usually a reward for winning the previous hole.

Hook: This is referred to as a shot that unintentionally curves excessively in a direction behind the hitter. It can be caused by several factors, but it is usually a miss hit.

Hosel: This is the part of a club connecting the shaft to the clubhead.

Hybrid Club: This type of club is fairly new and is a cross between an iron and a fairway wood. The hybrids usually replace the longer irons or fairway woods.

(I)

Integrity: The act of one doing the right thing based on their convictions, regardless of the outcome.

Impact: The moment in the swing when the club strikes the ball.

Interlocking Grip: This is a grip in which the pinky of the rear-hand and the index finger of the forward-hand weave into each other, thus promoting the palms opposing each other more when gripping the club. It allows the player to feel as though their hands are connected. This grip is preferred by many of the top players in the world.

In-to-Out Path: This is a term referring to the path of the club through the impact zone, relative to the target line as well as the alignment of the body. Depending on the angle of the clubface at the point of contact, the strike will produce a spin on the ball, and curve as a result. If the face is pointing outward relative to the body, it will produce a "push shot."

Irons: Irons are typically the thinnest clubheads in your bag. A typical player's bag may have numerous irons numbered 3, 4, 5, 6, 7, 8, 9 and PW. Also included are LW, and GW. Irons with lower numbers have less loft, produce a lower trajectory ball flight and travel farther.

(K)

Knock-Down-Shot: A de-lofted shot intended to travel on a low trajectory flight, which is commonly used to go under objects or escape high winds. This is similar to a "Punch Shot."

(L)

Lag: This is a term used to describe when the player has loaded the club in the backswing, by establishing an angle between the forward arm and the club and coiling the body, then maintaining the angle during the downswing, until just before entering the impact zone. This is how energy is accumulated, then stored through "Lag," and released through the shot. It is similar to cracking a whip.

Lateral Hazard: A lateral hazard usually referred to as a water hazard, is an area considered to be unplayable, that runs in the same direction as the hole. There are rules in place which govern how the player should proceed when they enter this area.

Layup Shot: A shot that is intentionally hit short of the green or targeted area, meant to favorably position the ball for the next shot, or to avoid unnecessary risk.

Leading Edge: The leading edge is the lowest portion along the bottom of the clubface on an iron.

Lie: The term "Lie" is referred to as the place where the ball comes to rest after being struck. This can include in the fairway, in the rough, or in a bunker.

Lie Angle: This is a term referring to the amount of degrees established between the clubface and the shaft. This will vary from one player to another, depending on the player's height and posture. The bottom center of the clubhead should be touching the ground. This will avoid hitting the ball heel or toe deep.

Line: The intended path of the ball usually referred to, in the context of putting.

Line of Flight: The actual path of the ball after being struck.

Links: A stretch of ground beside the sea, upon which golf is played. These are usually low-lying grounds with salt resistant grasses.

Loaded Position: A dynamic position at the top of the backswing, ready to efficiently apply force in the downswing.

Lob Shot: A short, high shot usually played with a wedge which is designed to land softly.

Loft: The amount of vertical degrees above the horizontal line, or what would be considered as level ground leading to the horizon. Loft applied to the ball through the stroke, relative to the horizontal plane, will produce what is referred to as trajectory. Clubs are numbered numerically, based on the loft of the club.

(M)

Match Play: This is a form of competition in which a number of holes won or lost by a player, or team, instead of the number of strokes played will determine the winner.

Maximum Clubs: Fourteen is the maximum number of clubs allowed during a stipulated round.

Mulligan: The custom of hitting a second ball—without penalty—on a hole.

(O)

Off the Pace: This is a term used to determine the status of a player's standing, when being compared to the leading score in a given tournament.

Open Clubface: This is a term used when the clubface is aiming outward, relative to the target line or swing path.

Open Stance: This is a term used to describe the body alignment relative to the target line or swing path. When more of the front of the body is facing the target line than the back, it is said to be in an "open stance."

Out-to-In Path: This is a term used to describe the path of the club through the impact zone, relative to the target line and or the body alignment.

Out of Bounds: Any area, other than the designated boundaries of the course established by the committee.

Overlapping Grip: This is a grip in which the pinky of the rear hand overlaps the area between the index and middle fingers of the forward hand, thus promoting the palms opposing each other more when gripping the club. This is also known as the" Vardon Grip," and is a very popular grip used by tour players.

Over the Top: This is a term used when a player takes the club beyond the parallel position at the top of the backswing.

(P)

Pace: The speed of the golf swing or the speed of the greens.

Par: Number of strokes assigned to a hole, that a player should be expected to score on a hole.

Parallel Position: This is a term referring to certain positions during the swing, which the club is parallel to the ground.

P.A.T.: Acronym for "*Player Ability Test.*"

Penalty: The addition of strokes to the scorecard as a result of a violation.

PGA: Acronym for "*Professional Golfers' Association.*"

Pin: A movable device, also referred to as a **Flag stick**, used to mark the exact location of the cup on the green.

Pin High: A ball is said to be "Pin High" on the green when it has been played as far as the placement of the hole or pin, and any distance either side. It is also known as hole high.

Pitch: A short distance shot onto the green, where the ball travels farther in the air than on the ground.

Plugged Lie: A situation where the ball remains in the indentation, or plug mark it makes when it lands.

Plumb-Bob: A method many players use to help them determine the amount a putt will break. When you position yourself behind the ball and hold the putter vertically, so it covers the ball, the shaft of the putter will indicate how much the ball will break.

Plus Handicap: A handicap less than the scratch score of the course.

Posture: Word used to describe the overall body angles at address. It is the infrastructure or frame work of the swing. This is the part of the swing where the hitter aligns the levers of the body, and establishes a balanced position.

Pre-Shot Routine: This is the point-in-time that the hitter gathers relevant information, determines his options, and then commits to the shot.

Punch Shot: A low-flying shot played with an abbreviated backswing and finish. The key to the shot is having the hands ahead of the ball at impact, which de-lofts the club.

(R)

Release: The unhinging of the angel established between the forward (dominant) hand and the club just prior to impact. There are actually two releases, the second being the rotation of the clubhead through impact.

Relief: The ability to move the position of the ball without penalty due to interference by an immovable obstruction, animal, ground condition or wrong putting green.

Reverse Pivot: The transfer of weight away from the target during the swing.

Rhythm: The coordination of movement during the golf swing or putting stroke.

Rough: Any playable area on the course other than the fairway, or a designated hazard.

(S)

Sand Trap: Also referred to as a "bunker," consisting of sand or grass or both that exists as an obstacle, and commonly referred to as a hazard.

Sand Wedge: An extremely lofted club with a wide flange, designed for playing from bunkers. The wide flange bounces the clubhead through the sand.

Scratch: A term used to describe the average score of a person with a zero handicap, also known as a "par golfer."

Setup: The process of addressing the ball, so that the club and body are properly aimed and aligned.

Shaft: The straight part of the club that connects the grip to the clubhead. Typically, made of metal or graphite.

Shaft Flex: Shaft Flex is defined as how much the shaft bends or gives in a back and forth manner. The flex designation printed on the shaft only pertains to that particular shaft model. What is stiff to one model made not be stiff to another. Picking the shaft type and model, therefore should be the first step on shaft fitting, even before flex.

Shank: A missed-hit stroke in which the ball is usually struck with the hosel or socket of the club.

Shape: To curve a shot to fit the situation. This word is also used to describe the flight of the ball.

Sky: A high, short shot caused by the clubhead striking the underside of the ball. Also known as a "pop-up."

Slice: A shot that severely curves in an outward direction, relative to the swing path.

Slot: A term used to describe the idea position at the top of the backswing, in which the club is set and ready, for the downswing.

Sole: When referring to equipment, this is the bottom of a club. When referring to the swing, it is the point when the sole of the club touches the ground at address.

Stance: The process of standing to the ball in readiness to hit a shot, as in "taking your stance."

Static Weight: The actual weight of the club in a vertical position.

Stroke Play: A form of competition based on the cumulative number of strokes taken, either over one round or several.

Surlyn: A thermal plastic resin similar to natural balata, used in ball manufacturing. It is a resilient material used for the cover of golf balls.

Swaying: An exaggerated, lateral movement of the body on either the backswing, forward swing, or both, which results in inconsistent shot making.

Swing Path: The direction the club is swung, relative to the target line.

Sweet Spot: The center and optimum hitting area of the clubface, that delivers the maximum possible mass behind the ball.

Swing Plane: The path that the hands and club travel around the spine or core axis.

(T)

Takeaway: The movement of the club at the beginning of the backswing.

Tangent: A force attempting to move in a straight line when a mass is moving in an arc, such as a clubhead during the swing.

Target Line: An imaginary line draw from the golf ball to the designated target.

Tee: The peg used to elevate the ball on the first shot of each hole.

Tee Ground: Also referred to as a "teeing area," or "tee box." It is the starting place for the hole to be played. The teeing area will vary, depending on the placement of the movable markers. The teeing ground consists of a rectangular area two club-lengths in depth from the markers.

Tempo: The speed and rhythmic motion made by the body during the golf swing while maintaining balance.

Timing: The sequence of motions within the golf swing.

Toed Shot: Any shot hit off the toe of the club.

Topped: A stroke in which the club strikes the top half of the ball in the shot.

Topped Spin: A term relevant in putting, where the top of the ball is moving in the direction of the target and the ball is said to be traveling on a true path.

Torsional Stiffness or Torque: This is simply the twist of a shaft when swung by a golfer. A composite shaft will generally undergo more twisting than steel. There are however, some composite shafts with a lesser torsional stiffness than even steel. The lower the rating, the lower the amount of twisting when put under stress. These are typically your higher grade shafts, which are tighter woven and feel harder and stiffer.

Trajectory: The angel of flight that a ball travels after being struck, and is measure in degrees relative to a horizontal line.

(U)

Upright Swing: A swing where the player moves the club well above shoulder level in the backswing, toward the head rather than the shoulder joint.

USGA: An acronym for "*United States Golf Association.*"

(V)

Vardon Grip: Also known as an "overlap grip." This is a grip in which the pinky of the rear hand overlaps the area between the index and middle fingers of the forward hand, thus promoting the palms opposing each other more when gripping the club. This is a very popular grip used by tour players.

Velocity: The speed of a golf ball.

Visualization: A mental image of a swing or shot, prior to actually executing it. This is typically part of the pre-shot routine.

(W)

Waggle: A swinging movement made with a golf club to and from over the ball prior to a stroke. It's a movement designed to eliminate tension in the arms and hands.

Wedge: A "wedge" is a highly lofted club typically used for hitting the shortest shots in golf. This club usually has an "S", "W", "L", or "G" on it.

Weight Shift: The transfer of weight from one side of the body to the other.

Whiff: A stroke at the ball which makes no contact with anything.

(X)

X-Factor: Is the intersection of imaginary lines, representing the spine angle and the swing plane. *See Posture*

(Y)

Yips: A psychological condition caused by nerves, resulting in a jerky motion during a putting stroke.

ABOUT THE AUTHORS

Chris Warner was introduced to the game of golf in 1970, at the age of nine, while caddying for his grandfather at a par-3 course in Jacksonville, Florida. He played through high school and into his adulthood. In 1995, Chris moved to Houston, Texas, and in 1996, he was employed by Continental Airlines, where he worked his way up to a position of Hub Manager. In 2003, he began taking Real Estate classes eventually acquiring his license in Texas. He accomplished his level (1) Affiliate, level (II) Associate, level III Full certification, and then level (IV) Master Teaching certification with the United States Golf Teacher's Federation. In addition, he completed the Field Examiners certification. Chris is a lifetime member of the PGA Tour Partners Club and is certified as a PGA and International PGA Instructor. Additionally, he is a certified teaching professional with the National Registry of Professional Golf Instructors and is a continuous member of the USGA and R&A United States Golf Association and Royal and Ancient. Chris has been named "Top 100 Teachers in the World" with the World Golf Teachers Federation. During his career, he has participated in numerous charities and fundraising events, helping to support the special needs organizations and teach the underprivileged students.

Lyn, born and raised Gwendolyn Ann Hudson, is a native of Louisiana and the daughter of a Methodist minister, Rev. Howard L. Hudson. After high school graduation, she attended college at U.S.L. in Lafayette, Louisiana, prior to moving to Houston, Texas. In 1996, she acquired a Texas Real Estate License and has remained in the industry ever since. Additionally, she was employed by Continental Airlines, and gave over fourteen years of dedicated service. She has two sons Clayton and Lance Lemmons, which have become avid golfers as well. Her passion has always been for children, as well as the under-privileged, while continuously contributing to their betterment. Through the years, she has participated in multiple charity fund raising events. Her desire is to someday create a foundation, introducing children to the game of golf, while giving every child the opportunity to enjoy the game, regardless of their social or financial status. Her commitment and drive as well as support for Chris' passion for golf, were key motivators for this book. The combination of talents and desire to help other people is a shared commitment between the couple.

TIGERS

RAZR

PUMA

PGA
RESORT AND SPA
PGA NATIONAL
PALM BEACH GARDENS

Titleist
2nd Annual Chrysalis Benefit Golf Tournament
CHRYSALIS
1st Place Team
PGA
SOUTHERN TEXAS SECTION